Inspirational Wit and Wisdom from the Internet

Inspirational Wit and Wisdom from the Internet

VOLUME ONE

by Dave Balsiger
and
Chris Strong

Bridge-Logos

Orlando, Florida 32822

Bridge-Logos

Orlando, FL 32822 USA

Inspirational Wit & Wisdom from the Internet
by Dave Balsiger and Chris Strong

Library of Congress Catalog Card Number: 2006904530
International Standard Book Number 0-88270-088-X

G1.316.N.m606.35250

Dedication

This book is dedicated to everyone who occasionally needs an inspirational uplift in their daily life – whether it be a time of laughter, a moment of reflection, or the shedding of tears that brings renewed joy to the heart.

This book is also dedicated to God who over my lifetime has been my inspiration to write, to produce television shows, and to speak out in the desire to make our world a little better place in which to live. God has always walked beside me, with me and before me in guiding my life's path in both the good and bad times. He has often enlightened me to a truth through the wit and wisdom of the literary gems contained in this book and on the CD.

Dave Balsiger

To my cousin, Pam Thornburg, who has inspired me with her personal wit and wisdom to become a better friend, a better mother, a better wife, and a woman of integrity. I have enjoyed a unique friendship with her that has made our long family history together richer over the years. She has given me her love and support through tears, joys and triumphs ... and, oh yes ... she has forwarded many inspirational stories to me from the Internet. Without people like Pam, who cherish these beautiful stories, there would be no book.

Chris Strong

Acknowledgments

I wish to express my deep appreciation to Joette Whims for her organizational and editing assistance. This book could not have been done without her dedicated help. Also, thanks to Ina Stacy-Shearin for her final edit on this book.

I'd also like to express my appreciation to Ann Strauss, my loyal executive assistant, who was always willing day or night to take on last minute assignments relating to this book.

Disclaimer of Rights

Invitation for Submissions

The Authors invite other writers to submit passages that they have authored for possible inclusion in future volumes of *Inspirational Wit and Wisdom from the Internet*. If you have recounted something that has happened in your life or created a short story that has inspired or entertained your friends and loved ones, we may be able to help you share your story with a greater audience. Authors typically pay writers between $50 and $250 (depending on length) for submissions that are included in the book. You may contact the Authors by writing to David W. Balsiger, P.O. Box 1987, Loveland, CO 80539-1987.

Table of Contents

Introduction   **xiii**

1   Maintaining Your Buddy List   **1**

Your Buddy List is Priceless   *2*

Stories of Friendship   *4*

Friendship Proverbs   *10*

Building Friendships   *13*

2   Remembering Favorite Places   **15**

Take a Trip Worth Remembering   *16*

Senior Wisdom   *17*

The Wisdom of Aging   *19*

Looking Back   *25*

Humor for the Over-the-Hill Gang   *27*

3   The Virtual Family Circle   **31**

Are You Dizzy Yet?   *33*

Family Matters   *34*

Kid Talk   *40*

The Cyberspace Classroom   *46*

The Family Pet   *51*

Leaving a Legacy   *52*

4   She's PC; He's Mac: The Gender Gap   **55**

Recognizing Our Differences   *56*

The South Pole   *57*

The North Pole   *61*

5 Click Here for Help   **69**

   Help is On the Way   *71*

   Tips for Healthy Living   *72*

   Food for the Soul   *77*

   Pointers from Nature   *82*

   Virtual Priorities   *84*

   Passions for Life   *86*

   Life's Issues   *90*

6 The Poetry Icon   **97**

   The Lost Art of Reading Poetry   *98*

   The Poetry Experience   *99*

7 Password: Special Days   **103**

   Making Memories   *104*

   Log on to the Holidays   *105*

   Remembering 9/11   *107*

   Other Special Days   *112*

8 Prayer: Message Board to Heaven   **117**

   Where Do Your Prayers Go?   *118*

   Prayer Stories   *119*

   Prayers for Today   *125*

   Prayer Purposes   *127*

9 FAQs for the Inspirational Side of Life   **131**

   What Do You Want to Know?   *133*

   Advice from God   *134*

   Wisdom for Living   *136*

   Keeping It in Perspective   *140*

Words to Remember   146
Stories to Live By   152
Tips for a Fuller Life   157

10 Access Amazing Stories   **161**
The Value of a Window   163
Windows into the Soul   164
Stories of Incredible Faith   168
Miracles of Love   171
Science Speaks God's Language   178
Kindness Conquers   180
God Is Still There   185

11 Church Chuckles   **195**
Just One More Laugh   197
Creative Creation   198
Theology 101   201
Who Is Jesus?   204
The Gospel According to Kids   207
Church Life   210
The Pearly Gates   217
Church Humor   220

About the Authors   **225**

Introduction

You've Got Mail!

It all started with a colossal failure and a project run amok. Miraculously, it morphed into a system of instantaneously exchanging messages and information around the world. What is it? The Internet, of course! For millions of us, it's the sound of connecting with those we love, admire, or need to ask for information. Right now, in millions of places, the greeting chimes, "You've got mail!"

Have you ever wondered how it all got started? Was it the genius of an entrepreneur who made millions on a patent, or the brain trust of scientists working in a prestigious lab in a famous university?

Neither of these. Just as the true depth of the Internet is an enigma, so the history of its development is a mysterious pathway. The first man credited with inventing a digital "computer" was Charles Babbage. In 1812, he was commissioned by the British government to invent a system for calculating the complex rise and fall of the tides worldwide. Babbage was gripped with the idea of creating a machine that could do intricate mathematical calculations accurately and quickly. He had a farsighted vision that we are just realizing today. He eventually developed a machine with 50,000 gear wheels. His invention was a failure because the technology of his day couldn't support the intricacies of his machine. What he set out to do seemed impossible to accomplish. He died an embittered old man.

Of course, you probably can guess what happened over the next 100 years. By the mid 1900s, advances in technology made it possible to build an electronic computer. The first, ENIAC, weighed more than 30 tons and took up 3,000 cubic feet of space. Yet it could not compute as well as a laptop computer of today! Can you imagine installing a "desktop" computer like that in your home? You'd have to build a massive room onto your home or business, install a special cooling system, and hire a team of experts to run it. Fortunately, computers have come a long way!

But another piece of the puzzle had to be put into place before a person in China could communicate in an instant with a business associate in Venezuela. This was a network of servers available for sending messages. This is the "run amok" part of the story. It all started in the 1960s when the U.S. Department of Defense decided it had a big problem. If the Army built one massive computer network, to which they would connect thousands of its machines, one well-placed enemy bomb could knock out the entire American defense communications system. So the DOD set up a web of networks and made them compatible with each other. This web soon sent shoots outside the government walls and kept spreading into every part of the globe. Today, students, researchers, businesses, educators, libraries, government officials, and millions of friends are linked into the World Wide Web.

The growth of the Internet has been phenomenal and continues to expand at lightning speed. Here are some fascinating facts about the Internet:

• More than one billion people worldwide use it from their homes, offices, and schools; 24 percent (or nearly 223 million) of these are Americans.

• You can search in more than 200 million sites, with 235,000 being added each month.

• The reach of the Internet as a source of information in the U.S. has increased from 60 to 70 percent of total households (this is equal to traditional newspapers).

• In the U.S., there are about 200 million e-mailboxes, 109 million of these are for business users and 90 million for consumer use.

• Internet penetration into U.S. households has reached nearly 75 percent, rising roughly 9 percentage points in a year.

• In the year 2000, more than 7 trillion e-mails were sent.

• Nearly 50 percent of the U.S. population communicates by e-mail.

• Fifty-eight million Americans sent e-mail daily in 2005, while 35 million used the Web to get news.

• Today, two out of every three Americans spend time online.

• The average e-mail user receives 31 e-mails per day.

How often do you become part of this Web? Once a week? Once a day? Many times a day?

Where do you log on? At home? At work? In a library? At school? In your bedroom? Even in your car? That's the beauty of the Internet's capability—we can access information and friends at any time of the day in almost any place!

What's so awesome about the story of the Internet is that it wasn't created by one person or one company—or even by one country. It's a product of all kinds of people working in their corners of the world to make communication more accessible and fun.

And that's the same way that the Internet works for us. It services all kinds of people working in their corners of the world to communicate in whatever way they want. No one has a patent on its process. No one can limit its reach.

We've come a long way, baby! From rural backyard news-gathering to Pony Express to airmail to e-mail. And something amazing has happened along the way. Besides the personal and business communication, the Web has also woven a tapestry of incredible stories, phenomenal news events, friendly chatter, handy tips, helpful office hints, astute family counsel, and riotous humor that pass from one person to the next with incredible speed. Many are inspirational stories or thoughts that make us weep, laugh aloud at the foibles of human nature, or think deeply about the ideals we hold dear. These messages, usually stamped with *Fwd:* in the subject box, find their way into thousands of e-mail inboxes. Many times, they seem to arrive at the very moment we need them. And they invariably make the world seem a little smaller, friendlier, and a warmer place to live.

In this book, we have collected some of the most outstanding examples of e-mail chatter and facts. Here you will find advice and information on almost every subject:
- How to win the battle of the sexes
- What's wrong and right in our political milieu
- What's good about our country
- The ins and outs of office relationships
- Belly laughs and one-liners
- How to find romance
- Inspirational stories about courageous people

When reading this book, perhaps you will read a few selections that have come across your own virtual inbox. Some may be so memorable that you have saved them in your computer's filing cabinet. Others may be new and may strike your funny bone or touch a tender spot in your heart. And some may just fit a situation you are facing right now.

We hope that reading these selections will inspire you, cause you to laugh, make you shake your head at human foolishness, cause you to stop and think, lift your mood and spirits, or maybe even motivate you to make a life change.

Along with the printed copy of the Internet messages, this book contains a CD with all these selections and many, many more so that you can pass along the stories and advice or humor that you think friends, family, or colleagues will enjoy.

Browse through the Table of Contents to find areas that interest you most. Bookmark the selections you find most appealing. Then forward them on to your best friend, your mate, your colleague, or your children. You'll have the pleasure of knowing that they, too, will hear, "You've got mail!"

Dave Balsiger and Chris Strong

Maintaining Your Buddy List

1

Your Buddy List is Priceless

Stories of Friendship
The Window
The Red Marble
A Friend in Need

Friendship Proverbs
Friends Are Forever
Good Friends Are ...
Thirty-three Friendship Proverbs

Building Friendships
Appreciate Life, Friend
A Friend Is Someone ...
Special People

Your Buddy List Is Priceless

The moment was etched in her mind like battery acid spilled on metal. Jill had opened a note that had fallen from her husband's wallet and found a love letter from his coworker. That small, pink piece of paper had plunged her family in chaos, resulting in a divorce and more heartbreak than she had ever dreamed was possible. Although she had tried her best to reconcile the situation, now her best friend of twenty-five years was married to another woman.

When it all happened, she didn't know where to turn or what to do. Within a few short months, her finances were shredded, her two children were acting out their pain in their individual ways, and her circle of friends had shrunk to just three.

But those three friends were made of gold. They had been there for her when she was at her lowest. Linda had cared for Jill's kids while she took a weekend off to get away from the pressure. Jenny had spent long hours patiently listening on the telephone during the hours when Jill felt she couldn't go on any longer. And Heather had brought over casseroles and canned goods when Jill's cupboards were bare. They had taken her out for coffee, spirited her away for a shopping spree, and invited her over during the holidays, which were now so painful for Jill, her son, and her daughter.

That had all happened over the past year. Although Jill's heart was still tender and scarred, she finally felt she was going to make it through the crisis. She and her children were beginning to settle into their new lives. She gave most of the credit for her family's emotional health to her three friends.

Jill didn't have money to buy the trio expensive gifts to show how much she appreciated their love and care. Also, she knew they didn't want showy displays of gratitude, but Jill needed to do something that told them how much she valued their friendship.

Then one night when she logged onto the Internet, she found an e-mail from a cousin in a distant city. It simply said:

Friends are angels who lift us to our feet
when our wings have trouble remembering how to fly.

That one sentence was exactly what she wanted to say, expressing her feelings in a way that she could never relate through a thousand words. With a spring in her heart, she clicked the "forward" button on the e-mail message and typed in her friends' e-mail addresses. Then she sat back and watched as the sentiment instantly flew to her friends' e-mail boxes.

Sure, she'd still try to find some little knickknacks to give her friends, and she'd still send thank-you notes occasionally. But for now, she felt thrilled and at peace with the message she was able to send.

Friendship is a delicate flower that can wilt without attention. That's how the Internet can prove invaluable. Frequent messages that say, "I appreciate you," link us with each other and keep our relationships vibrant. Through thoughtful forwards, we can maintain our "buddy list" and keep our friends informed of how we feel about them.

How is your buddy list? Do your friends receive daily or weekly communications from you that lift their spirits? Do you have a continuing conversation over the Internet with a few select friends who mean a lot to you?

Maintaining your buddy list is easy when you have the right messages at hand. Many of the ones included in this section will touch your heart deeply or will bring a chuckle as you picture your friends reading it. They are meant to keep that spark alive between those who have much in common and consider themselves committed friends.

Stories of Friendship

The Window

Two men, both seriously ill, occupied the same hospital room. One man was allowed to sit up in his bed for an hour each afternoon to help drain the fluid from his lungs. His bed was next to the room's only window. The other man had to spend all his time flat on his back.

The men talked for hours on end. They spoke of their wives and families, homes, jobs, involvement in military service, and where they had been on vacation.

Every afternoon when the man in the bed by the window could sit up, he would pass the time by describing to his immobile roommate all the things he could see outside the window. The grateful man in the other bed began to live for those one-hour periods when his mind would be broadened and enlivened by all the activity and color of the world outside. The window overlooked a park with a lovely lake. Ducks and swans played on the water while children sailed their model boats. Young lovers walked arm in arm amidst flowers of every color of the rainbow. Grand old trees graced the landscape, and a fine view of the city skyline could be seen in the distance.

As the man by the window described all this in exquisite detail, the bedridden man on the other side of the room would close his eyes and imagine the picturesque scene.

One warm afternoon, the man by the window described a parade passing by. Although the other man couldn't hear the band, he could see it in his mind's eye as the gentleman by the window portrayed it with very descriptive words.

Days and weeks passed. Then one morning, the day nurse arrived to bring water for their baths only to find the lifeless body of the man by the window. It appeared he had died peacefully in his sleep. She was saddened and called the hospital attendants to take the body away.

As soon as it seemed appropriate, the other man asked if he could now be moved next to the window. The nurse was happy to make the switch and after making sure he was comfortable, she left him alone. Slowly, painfully, he propped himself up on one elbow to take his first look at the world outside. Finally, he would have the joy of seeing it for himself. He strained to slowly turn to look out the window beside the bed. To his amazement, it faced a blank wall.

The man asked the nurse what could have compelled his deceased roommate to describe such wonderful things outside this window. "Perhaps he just wanted to encourage you," the nurse responded and further explained that the man was blind and could not even see the wall.

Moral: There is tremendous happiness in making others happy in spite of our own situations. Shared grief is half the sorrow, but happiness when shared, is doubled. If you want to feel rich, just count all the things you have that money can't buy.

"Today is a gift. That's why it is called the present."

The Red Marble

During the waning years of the depression in a small southeastern Idaho community, I used to stop by Mr. Miller's roadside stand for seasonal farm-fresh produce. Food and money were still extremely scarce and bartering was used extensively.

One particular day, while Mr. Miller was bagging some early potatoes for me, I noticed a small boy, delicate of bone and feature, ragged but clean, hungrily eyeing a basket of freshly picked green peas. I paid for my potatoes, but was also drawn to the display of fresh green peas. I am a pushover for creamed peas and new potatoes. As I pondered the peas, I couldn't help overhearing the conversation between Mr. Miller and the ragged boy next to me.

"Hello Barry, how are you today?"

"H'lo, Mr. Miller. Fine, thank ya. Jus' admirin' them peas. Sure look good."

"They are good, Barry. How's your Ma?"

"Fine. Gittin' stronger alla' time."

"Good. Anything I can help you with?"

"No, sir. Jus' admirin' them peas."

"Would you like to take some home?"

"No, sir. Got nuthin' to pay for 'em with."

"Well, what have you to trade me for some of those peas?"

"All I got's my prize marble here."

"Is that right? Let me see it."

"Here 'tis. She's a dandy."

"I can see that. Hmmmm, only thing is this one is blue and I sort of go for red. Do you have a red one like this at home?"

"Not 'zackley. But, almost."

"Tell you what. Take this sack of peas home with you, and next trip this way let me look at that red marble."

"Sure will. Thanks, Mr. Miller."

Mrs. Miller, who had been standing nearby, came over to help me. With a smile she said: "There are two other boys like him in our community, all three are in very poor circumstances. Jim just loves to bargain with them for peas, apples, tomatoes, or whatever. When they come back with their red marbles, and they always do, he decides he doesn't like red after all, so he sends them home with a bag of produce for a green marble or an orange one, perhaps."

I left the stand smiling to myself and impressed with this man.

A short time later I moved to Utah, but I never forgot the story of this man, the boys, and their bartering.

Several years went by, each one passing more rapidly than the previous one. Just recently, I had occasion to visit some old friends in that Idaho community and while I was there, I learned that Mr. Miller had died.

His viewing was that evening, and knowing my friends wanted to go, I agreed to accompany them. Upon our arrival at the mortuary, we took our place in line to meet the relatives of the deceased and to offer whatever words of comfort we could. Ahead of us in line were three young men. One was in an Army uniform, and the other two wore nice haircuts, dark suits, and white shirts. They were very professional looking.

They approached Mrs. Miller, who was smiling and composed by her husband's casket. Each of the young men hugged her and kissed her on the cheek, spoke briefly with her, then moved on to the casket. Her misty, light blue eyes followed them as, one by one, each young man stopped briefly to place his own warm hand over the cold pale hand in the casket. Each left the mortuary wiping his tear-filled eyes.

Our turn came to meet Mrs. Miller. I told her who I was and mentioned the story she had once told me about the marbles. With eyes glistening, she took my hand and led me to the casket. "Those three young men who just left were the same boys I told you about that day. They just told me how they appreciated the things Jim had 'traded' them."

"Now at last, when Jim could not change his mind about color or size, they each came to pay their debt."

"We've never had a great deal of the wealth of this world," she confided, "but right now, if alive, Jim would consider himself the richest man in Idaho."

With loving gentleness, she lifted the lifeless fingers of her deceased husband to find resting underneath were three, magnificently shiny, red marbles.

Moral: We will not be remembered as much by our words, as by our kind deeds.

A Friend in Need

One day, when I was a freshman in high school, I saw a kid named Kyle from my class walking home from school. It looked like he was carrying all of his books. I thought to myself, *"Why would anyone bring home all his books on a Friday? He must really be a nerd."*

I had quite a weekend planned (parties and a football game with my friend Saturday afternoon), so I shrugged my shoulders and went on. As I continued walking, I saw a bunch of kids running toward Kyle. They ran into him, knocking all the books out of his arms and tripping him so that he landed in the dirt. His glasses went flying and landed in the grass about ten feet from him.

He looked up, and I saw this terrible sadness in his eyes. My heart went out to him, so I jogged over to help him. As he crawled around on the ground with teary eyes, looking for his glasses, I handed him the glasses and said, "Those guys are jerks. They really should get lives."

He looked at me with a big smile on his face and said, "Hey thanks!" It was one of those smiles that showed real gratitude.

I helped him pick up his books and asked where he lived. As it turned out, he lived near me, so I asked why I had never seen him before. He said he had gone to private school before now.

We talked all the way home as I carried his books. He turned out to be a pretty cool kid. I asked him if he wanted to play football on Saturday with my friends and me. He said yes. We hung out all weekend, and the more I got to know Kyle, the more I liked him. And my friends thought the same of him. Until then, I would have never hung out with a private school kid before.

Monday morning came, and there was Kyle with the huge stack of books again. I stopped him and said, "Boy, you are gonna really build some serious muscles with this pile of books everyday!" He laughed and handed me half the books.

Over the next four years, Kyle and I became best friends. When we were seniors, we began to think about college. Kyle decided on Georgetown, and I was going to Duke. He was going to be a doctor, and I was going for business on a football scholarship. I knew that we would always be friends, that the miles would never be a problem.

Kyle was valedictorian of our class, and I teased him all the time about being a nerd. He had to prepare a speech for graduation. I was so glad that I didn't have to get up and speak.

Graduation day came, and Kyle looked great. He was one of those guys who really found himself during high school. He filled out and actually looked good in glasses. He had more dates than I did, and all the girls loved him! Sometimes I was jealous, and today was one of those days. I could see that he was nervous about his speech, so I smacked him on the back and said, "Hey, big guy, you'll be great."

He looked at me with one of those looks (the really grateful one) and smiled. "Thanks," he said.

As he started his speech, he cleared his throat and began. "Graduation is a time to thank those who helped you make it through those tough years—your parents, your teachers, your siblings, maybe a coach, but mostly your friends. I am here to tell all of you that being a friend to someone is the best gift you can give them. I am going to tell you a story."

I just looked at my friend in disbelief as he told the story of the first day we met. He shared how he had planned to kill himself over that weekend. He talked of how he had cleaned out his locker so that his Mom wouldn't have to do it later and was carrying his stuff home. He looked directly at me and gave me a little smile. "Thankfully, I was saved. My friend saved me from doing the unspeakable."

I heard a gasp go through the crowd as this handsome, popular boy told us about his weakest moment. I saw his Mom and Dad looking at me and smiling that same grateful smile. Not until that moment did I realize its depth.

Never underestimate the power of your actions. With one small gesture, you can change a person's life—for better or for worse. God puts us all in each other's lives to impact one another in some way. Look for God in others.

Friendship Proverbs

Friends Are Forever

Life is short, so enjoy your walk through it.

Love starts with a smile, grows with a kiss, and ends with a tear.

Don't cry over anyone who won't cry over you.

If love isn't a game, why are there so many players?

Good friends are hard to find, harder to leave, and impossible to forget.

You can only go as far as you push.

Actions speak louder than words.

The hardest thing to do is to watch the one you love, love someone else.

Don't let the past hold you back. You're missing the good stuff.

Life's short. If you don't look around once in a while, you might miss it.

A best friend is like a four-leaf clover—hard to find and lucky to have.

Some people make the world special just by being in it.

Best friends are the siblings God forgot to give us.

When it hurts to look back, and you're scared to look ahead, you can look beside you and your best friend will be there.

True friendship never ends.
Friends are forever.

Good Friends Are ...

Good friends are like stars. You don't always see them, but you know they are always there.

Don't frown. You never know who is falling in love with your smile.

What do you do when the only person who can make you stop crying is the person who made you cry?

No one is perfect until you fall in love with him or her.

Everything is okay in the end. If it's not okay, then it's not the end.

Most people walk in and out of your life, but only friends leave footprints in your heart.

Friends are quiet angels who lift us to our feet when our wings have trouble remembering how to fly.

You may be only one person in the world, but to someone else you are the world.

Thirty-three Friendship Proverbs

1. To be a friend, just make yourself worth knowing.
2. Friends are those rare people who ask how we are and then wait to hear the answer.
3. If it breaks a friendship, it is not worth it.
4. True friends have hearts that beat as one.
5. If you cannot think of any nice things to say about your friends, don't speak at all.
6. Make friends before you need them.

7. If you were another person, would you like to be a friend of yours?

8. A good friend is one who neither looks down on you nor keeps up with you.

9. Be friendly with the folks you know. If it weren't for them, you would be a total stranger.

10. A friend is never known until he is needed.

11. Friendship is a responsibility, not an opportunity.

12. Friendship is the cement that holds the world together.

13. Friends are those who speak to you after others quit.

14. The reason a dog has so many friends is that he wags his tail and not his tongue.

15. Pick your friends, but not to pieces.

16. A friend is one who put his finger on a fault without rubbing it in.

17. The way to have friends is to be willing to lose some arguments.

18. If a friend makes a mistake, ignore it.

19. Deal with others' faults as gently as if they were your own.

20. People are judged by the company they keep and the company they keep away from.

21. A friend is a person who can step on your toes without messing up your shine.

22. The best mirror is an old friend.

23. The best possession one may have is a true friend.

24. Make friendship a habit and you will always have friends.

25. You will never have a friend unless you are a friend.

26. Doing nothing for your friends results in having no friends to do for.

27. Anyone can give advice; a real friend will lend a helping hand.

28. You can make more friends by being interested in them than trying to have them be interested in you.

29. A real friend is a person who, when you've made a fool of yourself, lets you forget it.

30. A friend is a person who listens attentively while you say nothing.

31. A friend is worth a fortune, but never in dollars.

32. True friends are like diamonds, precious but rare; false friends are like autumn leaves, found everywhere.

33. A friend is someone who thinks you're a good egg even though you're slightly cracked.

Building Friendships

Appreciate Life, Friend

Even though I clutch my blanket and growl when the alarm rings, thank You, Lord, that I can hear. There are many who are deaf.

Even though I keep my eyes closed against the morning light as long as possible, thank You, Lord, that I can see. Many are blind.

Even though I huddle in my bed and put off rising, thank You, Lord, that I have the strength to rise. There are many who are bedridden.

Even though the first hour of my day is hectic, when socks are lost, toast is burned, tempers are short, and my children are so loud, thank You, Lord, for my family. There are many who are lonely.

Even though our breakfast table never looks like the pictures in magazine and the menu is at time unbalanced, thank You, Lord, for the food we have. There are many who are hungry.

Even though the routine of my job is often monotonous, thank You, Lord, for the opportunity to work. There are many who have no job.

Even though I grumble and bemoan my fate from day to day and wish my circumstances were not so modest, thank You, Lord, for life!

A Friend Is Someone ...

A friend is someone we turn to when our spirits need a lift.
A friend is someone to treasure, for friendship is a gift.
A friend is someone who fills our lives with Beauty, Joy, and Grace.
And makes the world we live in a better and happier place.
YOU ARE MY FRIEND AND I AM HONORED!

Special People

It is said that it takes a minute to find a special person, an hour to appreciate him, a day to love him, but an entire life to forget him.

Remembering Favorite Places

2

Take a Trip Worth Remembering

Senior Wisdom
Not Our Responsibility
Yes, I'm a Senior Citizen

The Wisdom of Aging
Theories of Aging
Truths About Life
God Won't Ask ...
I've Learned ...

Looking Back
You Know You're Between...

Humor for the Over-the-Hill Gang
Still in the Box
Hymns for the Over-50 Crowd
Things My Mother Taught Me ...

Take a Trip Worth Remembering

When was the last time you sat in a lounge chair on your patio on a warm afternoon, and let your mind wander back through the past? As the cotton-ball clouds float above, your thoughts drift to a simpler, less hectic time. A breeze lightly caresses your arms and the iced tea at your side quenches your thirst. As you wander back, what do you see? Can you smell the lingering memories of your past? What do you hear? Are the sounds pleasant or raucous? Can you taste those familiar tastes? Your mother's favorite casserole, the tang of homemade lemonade, the salt water of the ocean. Do your fingers touch and your skin tingle?

If you are over twenty, you have stored in your memory a million favorite places. They are hidden, but within reach if you access them through a familiar image or the sounds of an old song. They are treasures buried deeply, waiting to be uncovered.

"Remembering Favorite Places" will help you access your choice memories and send them on to your friends and family who you know will savor them too. These memories can make the present come alive with the fragrances of the past.

And if you dare, you can travel further back than your own memories to the days of our ancestors. What was life like for them compared to our own lifestyles? What did they do that we no longer practice? What would amuse and amaze us about their lives? How has the minutia of daily life changed?

Now that your curiosity has been piqued, go on and read the selections in "Remembering Favorite Places." Take the exciting trip that won't cost you a dime! Then pass on the train ticket to the past to a friend.

Senior Wisdom

Not Our Responsibility

Senior citizens are constantly being criticized for every conceivable deficiency of the modern world, real or imaginary. We take responsibility for all we have done and do not blame others. But, upon reflection, we would like to point out that it was *not* the senior citizens who took:

The melody out of music,
The pride out of appearance,
The romance out of love,
The commitment out of marriage,
The responsibility out of parenthood,
The togetherness out of the family,
The learning out of education,
The service out of patriotism,
The Golden Rule from rulers,
The civility out of behavior,
The refinement out of language,
The dedication out of employment,
The prudence out of spending, or
The ambition out of achievement.

And we certainly are NOT the ones who eliminated patience and tolerance from personal relationships and interactions with others!

Does anyone under the age of 50 know the lyrics to the *Star Spangled Banner*? Just look at the seniors with tears in their eyes and pride in their hearts as they stand at attention with their hands over their hearts!

Remember—inside every older person is just a younger person wondering what the heck happened!

Yes, I'm a Senior Citizen

I'm the life of the party—even if it lasts until 8 p.m.

I'm very good at opening child-proof caps with a hammer.

I'm usually interested in going home before I get to where I am going.

I'm awake many hours before my body allows me to get up.

I'm smiling all the time because I can't hear a thing you're saying.

I'm very good at telling stories—over and over and over and over again.

I'm aware that other people's grandchildren are not nearly as cute as mine.

I'm so cared for—long-term care, eye care, private care, dental care.

I'm not grouchy; I just don't like traffic, waiting, crowds, or politicians.

I'm sure everything I can't find is in a secure place.

I'm wrinkled, saggy, lumpy, and that's just my left leg.

I'm having trouble remembering simple words like …

I'm realizing that aging is not for wimps.

I'm sure they are making adults much younger these days.

And when did they let kids become policemen?

I'm wondering: If you're as old as you feel, how can I be alive at 150?

I'm a walking storeroom of facts. I've just lost the key to the storeroom door.

Yes, I'm a Senior Citizen, and I think I am having the time of my life!

Now if I could only remember who sent this to me, I would send it to many more! Have I already sent this to you?

The Wisdom of Aging

Theories of Aging

"I never think of the future. It comes soon enough." –Albert Einstein

Age is a funny thing when you think about it! Do you realize that the only time in our lives when we like to get older is when we're kids? If you're less than 10 years old, you're so excited about getting older that you think in fractions. "How old are you?" "I'm four-and-*a-half*." You're four-and-a-half going on five! But as an adult, you're never 36-and-a-half, but barely thirty-six right up to your thirty-seventh birthday!

When you get into your teens, no one can hold you back. You jump to the next number. "How old are you?" "I'm gonna be 16." You could be 12, but you're gonna be 16.

And then comes the greatest day of your life. You become 21. Even the words sound like a ceremony. You *become* 21. *YES!*

But then you turn 30. Oops, what happened here? Makes you sound like bad milk. You *turned*; we had to throw you out. There's no fun now. What's wrong?

What changed? You *become* 21, you *turn* 30, and then you're *pushing* 40. Stay over there; it's beginning to slip away.

You *become* 21, you *turn* 30, then you're *pushing* 40, you *reach* 50, and then you *make it* to 60. I didn't think I'd make it, but I did.

You *become* 21, you *turn* 30, then you're *pushing* 40, you *reach* 50, and you *make it* to 60. By then, you build up so much speed that you *hit* 70!!!!!

Soon, it's a day-by-day thing. After that, you *hit* Wednesday. You get into your 80s, you *hit* lunch. And eventually it's an hour by hour thing—you're *turning* 4:30. My grandmother won't even buy green bananas. "Well, it's an investment, you know, and maybe a bad one."

But it doesn't end there. Into your 90s, you start going backwards. I was *just* 92.

Then a strange thing happens. If you make it over 100, you become like a little kid again. I'm 100-and-a-half!!!

Reprinted from *The Baby Boomers Guide to Living Forever*, by Terry Grossman, M.D., Golden, Colorado: Hubristic Press, 2000. Article by unknown author.

Truths About Life

Great Truths About Life That Adults Have Learned:

1. Raising teenagers is like nailing Jell-O to a tree.

2. Wrinkles don't hurt.

3. Families are like fudge—mostly sweet with a few nuts.

4. Today's mighty oak is just yesterday's nut that held its ground.

5. Laughing is good exercise. It's like jogging on the inside.

6. Middle age is when you choose your cereal for the fiber, not the toy.

Great Truths About Growing Old:

1. Growing old is mandatory; growing up is optional.

2. Forget the health food. You need all the preservatives you can get.

3. When you fall down, you wonder what else you can do while you're down there.

4. You're getting old when you get the same sensation from a rocking chair that you once got from a roller coaster.

5. It's frustrating when you know all the answers, but no one bothers to ask you any questions.

6. Time may be a great healer, but it's a lousy beautician.

7. Wisdom comes with age, but sometimes age comes alone.

The Four Stages of Life:
1. You believe in Santa Claus.
2. You don't believe in Santa Claus.
3. You are Santa Claus.
4. You look like Santa Claus.

Great Truths about Success:
At age 4, success is ... not peeing in your pants.
At age 12, success is ... having friends.
At age 16, success is ... having a driver's license.
At age 20, success is ... having sex.
At age 35, success is ... having money.
At age 50, success is ... having money.
At age 60, success is ... having sex.
At age 70, success is ... having a driver's license.
At age 75, success is ... having friends.
At age 80, success is ... not peeing in your pants.

God Won't Ask ...

God won't ask what kind of car you drove, *but He'll ask* how many people you drove who didn't have transportation.

God won't ask the square footage of your house, *but He'll ask* how many people you welcomed into your home.

God won't ask about the clothes you had in your closet, *but He'll ask* how many you helped to clothe.

God won't ask about your social status; *but He'll ask* what kind of class you displayed.

God won't ask how many material possessions you owned, *but He'll ask* how many owned you.

God won't ask what your highest salary was, *but He'll ask* if you lowered your values to obtain it.

God won't ask how much overtime you worked, *but He'll ask* if the overtime work was for yourself or for your family.

God won't ask how many promotions you received, *but He'll ask* you how you promoted others.

God won't ask what your job title was, *but He'll ask* if you performed your job to the best of your ability.

God won't ask what you did to help yourself, *but He'll ask* what you did to help others.

God won't ask how many friends you had, *but He'll ask* how many people to whom you were a friend.

God won't ask what you did to protect your rights, *but He'll ask* what you did to protect the rights of others.

God won't ask in what neighborhood you lived, *but He'll ask* how you treated your neighbors.

God won't ask about the color of your skin, *but He'll ask* about the content of your character.

God won't ask how many times your deeds matched your words, *but He'll ask* about the times they didn't.

God won't ask why it took so long to seek salvation, *but He'll lovingly take* you to your mansion in heaven, and not to the gates of hell.

God won't ask how many people you forwarded this too, *but He'll ask* if you were ashamed to pass it on to your friends.

I've Learned ...

I've learned ... that you cannot make someone love you. All you can do is be someone who can be loved. The rest is up to them.

I've learned ... that no matter how much I care, some people just don't care back.

I've learned ... that it takes years to build up trust, and only seconds to destroy it.

I've learned … that it's not what you have in your life but who you have in your life that counts.

I've learned … that you can get by on charm for about fifteen minutes. After that, you'd better know something.

I've learned … that you shouldn't compare yourself to the best others can do.

I've learned … that you can do something in an instant that will give you heartache for life.

I've learned … that it's taken me a long time to become the person I want to be.

I've learned … that you should always leave loved ones with loving words. It may be the last time you see them.

I've learned … that you can keep going long after you can't.

I've learned … that we are responsible for what we do, no matter how we feel.

I've learned … that either you control your attitude or it controls you.

I've learned … that regardless of how hot and steamy a relationship is at first, the passion fades and there had better be something enduring to take its place.

I've learned … that heroes are the people who do what has to be done when it needs to be done, regardless of the consequences.

I've learned … that money is a lousy way of keeping score.

I've learned … that my best friend and I can do anything or nothing, yet have the best time.

I've learned … that sometimes the people you expect to kick you when you're down will be the ones to help you get back up.

I've learned … that sometimes when I'm angry I have the right to be angry, but that doesn't give me the right to be cruel.

I've learned … that just because someone doesn't love you the way you want them to doesn't mean they doesn't love you with all they have.

I've learned … that maturity has more to do with what types of experiences you've had and what you've learned from them, and less to do with how many birthdays you've celebrated.

I've learned … that you should never tell a child his dreams are unlikely or outlandish. Few things are more humiliating, and what a tragedy it would be if he believed you.

I've learned … that your family won't always be there for you. It may seem funny, but people you aren't related to can take care of you, love you and teach you to trust people again. Families aren't only biological.

I've learned … that no matter how good a friend is, he is going to hurt you every once in a while and you must forgive him for that.

I've learned … that it isn't always enough to be forgiven by others. Sometimes you need to learn to forgive yourself.

I've learned … that no matter how bad your heart is broken, the world doesn't stop for your grief.

I've learned … that our background and circumstances may have influenced who we became, but we are responsible for who we are.

I've learned … that just because two people argue, it doesn't mean they don't love each other. And just because they don't argue, it doesn't mean they do.

I've learned … that we don't have to change friends if we understand that friends change.

I've learned … that you shouldn't be so eager to find out a secret. It could change your life forever.

I've learned … that two people can look at the exact same thing and see something totally different.

I've learned … that no matter how you try to protect your children, they will eventually get hurt and you will hurt in the process.

I've learned … that your life can be changed in a matter of hours by people who don't even know you.

I've learned … that even when you think you have no more to give, when a friend cries out to you, you will find the strength to help.

I've learned … that credentials on the wall do not make you a decent human being.

I've learned … that sometimes the people you care about most in life are taken from you too soon.

I've learned … that one must learn to determine where to draw the line between being nice and not hurting people's feelings and standing up for what you believe.

Looking Back

You Know You're Lost Between a Baby Boomer and a Generation X'er if …

1. You remember when Jordache jeans with a flat handle comb in the back pocket were cool.

2. In your class picture, you're wearing an Izod shirt with the collar up.

3. You know by heart the words to any Weird Al Yankovic song.

4. You ever rang someone's doorbell and said, "Landshark!"

5. Three words: ATARI, IntelliVision, and Coleco, sound familiar.

6. You remember the premier of MTV. In fact, you remember the Friday night videos before the days of MTV.

7. A predominant color in your childhood photos is plaid.

8. While in high school, you and your friends discussed elaborate plans to get together again at the end of the century and play Prince's 1999 until you passed out partying.

9. You remember when music labeled "alternative" really was alternative. And when alternative comedy really was funny.

10. You took family trips *before* the invention of the minivan.

11. You rode in the back of the station wagon, and you faced the cars behind you.

12. You've recently horrified yourself by using any one of the following phrases: When I was younger ... When I was your age ... You know, back when ...

13. Schoolhouse Rock played a *huge* part in how you actually learned the English language.

14. You ever dressed to emulate a person you saw in a Duran Duran, Madonna, or Cyndi Lauper video.

15. The first time you ever kissed someone at a dance came during either *Crazy for You* or *Leather and Lace*.

16. You remember with pain the sad day when the Green Machine hit the streets and made the Big Wheel obsolete.

17. The phrase, "Where's the beef," still doubles you over with laughter.

18. You honestly remember when film critics raved that no movie could ever possibly get better special effects than those in the movie, *Tron*.

19. You had a crush on either Ted, the photographer on *The Love Boat*, Gage from *Emergency*, or Ponch, the motorcycle cop from *Chips*.

20. Your hair at some point in time in the 80s became something that can only be described by the phrase; "I was experimenting."

21. You've shopped at a Benetton.

22. You know the difference between Pinky Tuscadero and Leather Tuscadero.

23. You wore leg warmers over your jeans.

Humor for the Over-the-Hill Gang

Still in the Box

"Computers in the future may weigh no more than 1.5 tons." —
Popular Mechanics, forecasting the relentless march of science,
1949

"I think there is a world market for maybe five computers." —
Thomas Watson, chairman of IBM, 1943

*"I have traveled the length and breadth of this county and talked
with the best people, and I can assure you that data processing is a
fad that won't last out the year."* —The editor in charge of business
books for Prentice Hall, 1957

"But what … is it good for?"—Engineer at the Advanced
Computing Systems Division of IBM, 1968, commenting on the
microchip

*"There is no reason anyone would want a computer in their
home."*—Ken Olson, president, chairman, and founder of Digital
Equipment Corp., 1977

*"This 'telephone' has too many shortcomings to be seriously
considered as a means of communication. The device is inherently
of no value to us."*—Western Union internal memo, 1876

*"The wireless music box has no imaginable commercial value.
Who would pay for a message sent to nobody in particular?"*—
David Sarnoff's associates in response to his urgings for investment
in the radio in the 1920s

*"The concept is interesting and well-formed, but in order to
earn better than a 'C,' the idea must be feasible."*—A Yale
University management professor in response to Fred Smith's paper
proposing reliable overnight delivery service (Smith went on to
found Federal Express Corp.)

"Who the hell wants to hear actors talk?"—H. M. Warner,
Warner Brothers, 1927

"I'm just glad it'll be Clark Gable who's falling on his face and not Gary Cooper."—Gary Cooper on his decision not to take the leading role in *Gone with the Wind*

"A cookie store is a bad idea. Beside, the market research reports say Americans like crispy cookies, not soft and chewy cookies like you make."—Response to Debbi Fields' idea of starting Mrs. Fields' Cookies

"We don't like their sound; guitar music is on the way out."—Decca Recording Co. rejecting the Beatles, 1962

"Heavier-than-air flying machines are impossible."—Lord Kelvin, president, Royal Society, 1895

"If I had thought about it, I wouldn't have done the experiment. The literature was full of examples that said you can't do this."—Spencer Silver, on the work that led to the unique adhesives for 3-M "Post-It" Notepads

"So we went to Atari and said, 'Hey, we've got this amazing thing, even built with some of your parts, and what do you think about funding us? Or we'll give it to you. We just want to do it. Pay our salary, we'll come work for you.' And they said, 'No.' So then we went to Hewlett-Packard, and they said, 'Hey, we don't need you. You haven't got through college yet.'"—Apple Computer Inc. founder Steve Jobs on attempts to get Atari and HP interested in his and Steve Wozniak's personal computer

"Professor Goddard does not know the relation between action and reaction and the need to have something better than a vacuum against which to react. He seems to lack the basic knowledge ladled out daily in high schools."—1921 New York Times editorial about Robert Goddard's revolutionary rocket work

"You want to have consistent and uniform muscle development across all of your muscles? It can't be done. It's just a fact of life. You just have to accept inconsistent muscle development as an unalterable condition of weight training."—Response to Arthur Jones, who solved the "unsolvable" problem by inventing Nautilus

"Drill for oil? You mean drill into the ground to try and find oil? You're crazy." — Drillers who Edwin L. Drake tried to enlist to his project to drill for oil in 1859

"Stocks have reached what looks like a permanently high plateau." — Irving Fisher, Professor of Economics, Yale University, 1929

"Airplanes are interesting toys but of no military value." — Marechal Ferdinand Foch, Professor of Strategy, Ecole Superieure de Guerre

"Everything that can be invented has been invented." — Charles H. Duell, Commissioner, U.S. Office of Patents, 1899

"Louis Pasteur's theory of germs is ridiculous fiction." — Pierre Pachet, Professor of Physiology at Toulouse, France, 1872

"The abdomen, the chest, and the brain will forever be shut from the intrusion of the wise and humane surgeon." — Sir John Eric Ericksen, British Surgeon, appointed Surgeon-Extraordinary to Queen Victoria 1873

"640K ought to be enough for anybody." — Bill Gates

P.S. Feel like thinking big and "out of the box" now??!!

Hymns for the Over-50 Crowd

1. "Just a 'Slower' Walk with Thee"
2. "It Is Well with My Soul," But My Knees Hurt
3. "Nobody Knows the Trouble I 'Have Seeing'"
4. "Precious Lord, Take My Hand," and Help Me Up
5. "Count Your Many 'Birthdays,' Count Them One by One"
6. "Go Tell It On a Mountain," But Speak Up
7. "Give Me the 'Old Timers' Religion"
8. "Blessed 'Insurance'"
9. "Guide Me, O Thou Great Jehovah," I've Forgotten Where I've Parked the Car

Things My Mother Taught Me ...

Most of us can relate to these.

My mother taught me LOGIC

"If you fall off that swing and break your neck, you can't go to the store with me!"

My mother taught me about MEDICINE

"If you don't stop crossing your eyes, they're going to freeze that way."

My mother taught me TO THINK AHEAD

"If you don't pass your spelling test, you'll never get a good job!"

My mother taught me ESP

"Put your sweater on; don't you think that I know when you're cold?"

My mother taught me TO MEET A CHALLENGE

"What were you thinking? Answer me when I talk to you, don't talk back to me!"

My mother taught me about HUMOR

"When that lawn mower cuts off your toes, don't come running to me!"

My mother taught me about how to BECOME AN ADULT

"If you don't eat your vegetables, you will never grow up."

My mother taught me about GENETICS

"You are just like your father!"

My mother taught me about my ROOTS

"Do you think you were born in a barn?"

My mother taught me about the WISDOM OF AGE

"When you get to be my age, you will understand ... "

My mother taught me about ANTICIPATION

"Just wait 'til your father comes home."

My mother taught me about RECEIVING

"You are going to get it when your father comes home."

And the all time favorite: JUSTICE

"One day you will have kids and I hope they turn out just like YOU. Then you'll see what it's like!"

The Virtual Family Circle

3

Are You Dizzy Yet?

Family Matters
You Are My Sunshine
Your Children Are Watching
How to Know Whether ...
The Love Dress

Kid Talk
What Does Love Mean?
Goldfish
Freckles
Family Planning
Son, Get a Haircut
Kids Advice to Kids
My Dad Is Better Than Yours

The Cyberspace Classroom
Schoolroom Proverbs
The Blue Ribbon
Wisdom from Student Writings

The Family Pet
Dear Buddy

Leaving a Legacy
A Wise Investment
I Wish You Enough

Are You Dizzy Yet?

"Mama, Mama!"

Mama keeps talking on the telephone.

"Mama, Mama!"

Mama looks down at her preschooler and frowns, but keeps talking on the telephone.

"Mama, Mama!"

Finally, Mama turns to her child and says firmly, "What do you want?"

"Nothing," the child answers.

Family life is full of those daily occurrences that make parents want to pull out their hair. Little Johnny tries to see if his boat will float—in the toilet after he flushes. Call the plumber! Little Jennifer uses daddy's toothbrush to make the dog's breath smell fresher. If only she'd mentioned this to daddy before he brushed his teeth! Caleb put a password on the computer, but forgot what the password was. And this is the day Mother has to pay bills online!

If you have a family, you can put your own experiences on this list. These are the stories we pull out at family reunions and laugh over until our bellies hurt—but not until years later! These are the memories we take with us no matter where we go, the incidents that make the family circle spin.

Family memories can run from the moment that he asked her to marry him while they were bowling, to the night that Grandma gave each grandchild a pat and a loving word just before she went into surgery. Children, aunts, uncles, moms, dads, and grandparents all add to the dizzying milieu that makes up the family circle. And now you can extend that carnival ride to your cyberspace family. Are all of you hooked up to the Internet? Do you communicate with each other through cyberspace? With our lives so busy these days, what a joy to have a way to keep in contact that serves us conveniently and timely! Use your Internet Service Provider to encourage your family, to send a message of love, or to brighten someone's day with humor. Consider opening up a dialogue with your children and see how writing messages to them will change your relationship and open up areas of communication that were closed before.

If you have a memory that seems especially funny or poignant, write it down and slip the paper between the pages of this book at this spot. Then whenever you want to send a family member a warm note, include your story in your e-mail. Express to your loved one the humorous spin in your virtual family circle.

Family Matters

You Are My Sunshine

Like any good mother, when Karen found out that another baby was on the way, she did what she could to help her 3-year-old son, Michael, prepare for a new sibling. They found out that the new baby was going to be a girl, and day after day, night after night, Michael sang to his sister in Mommy's tummy. He was building a bond of love with his little sister before he even met her.

The pregnancy progressed normally for Karen, an active member of the Panther Creek United Methodist Church in Morristown, Tennessee. In time, the labor pains came. Soon they were every five minutes, every three, every minute. But serious complications arose during delivery, and Karen found herself in hours of labor. Would a C-section be required?

Finally, after a long struggle, Michael's little sister was born. But she was in very serious condition. With a siren howling in the night, the ambulance rushed the infant to the neonatal intensive care unit at St. Mary's Hospital, Knoxville, Tennessee.

The days inched by. The little girl got worse. The pediatrician had to tell the parents, "There is very little hope. Be prepared for the worst."

Karen and her husband contacted a local cemetery about a burial plot. They had fixed up a special room in their house for their new baby, but now they found themselves having to plan for a funeral. Michael, however, kept begging his parents to let him see his sister. "I want to sing to her," he kept saying.

Week two in intensive care looked as if a funeral would come before the week was over. Michael kept nagging about singing to his sister, but kids are never allowed in the Intensive Care Unit.

Karen decided to take Michael whether they liked it or not. If he didn't see his sister right then, he may never see her alive. She dressed him in an oversized scrub suit and marched him into ICU. He looked like a walking laundry basket.

The head nurse recognized him as a child and bellowed, "Get that kid out of here now! No children are allowed."

The "mother" in Karen rose up strong, and the usually mild-mannered lady glared steel-eyed right into the head nurse's face. With her lips a firm line, she stated, "He is not leaving until he sings to his sister." Then Karen towed Michael to his sister's bedside.

He gazed at the tiny infant losing the battle to live. After a moment, he began to sing. In the pure-hearted voice of a 3-year-old, Michael sang: "You are my sunshine, my only sunshine. You make me happy when skies are gray."

Instantly, the baby girl seemed to respond. The pulse rate began to calm down and become steady.

"Keep on singing, Michael," encouraged Karen with tears in her eyes.

"You never know, dear, how much I love you. Please don't take my sunshine away."

As Michael sang to his sister, the baby's ragged, strained breathing became as smooth as a kitten's purr.

"Keep on singing, sweetheart."

"The other night, dear, as I lay sleeping, I dreamed I held you in my arms."

Michael's little sister began to relax as rest, healing rest, seemed to sweep over her.

"Keep on singing, Michael."

Tears had now conquered the face of the bossy head nurse. Karen glowed.

"You are my sunshine, my only sunshine. Please don't take my sunshine away … "

The very next day, the little girl was well enough to go home.

Woman's Day Magazine called it "The Miracle of a Brother's Song."

The medical staff just called it a miracle. Karen called it a miracle of God's love.

Never give up on the people you love. Love is so incredibly powerful.

Life is good. Have a wonderful day!

Your Children Are Watching

All kids have video-camera eyes and audio-tape-recording ears. They see and hear everything we do and say—including what we don't do or say, but should.

How we live out our marriage has a lasting impact on them. If you have children at home, you're now training them how to be a future husband or wife—a future father or mother. The example your marriage sets will have a trickle-down effect on your son or daughter. If you're married but have no children yet, print this out and save for the day you do. Grown children gone? You can impact your grandchildren.

The Trickle Down Effect

• Show Affection to Each Other—Sitting close to one another, hand holding, hugging, and kissing give your kids security that you love each other and are in your marriage to stay.

• Extend Courtesies to Each Other—Saying "thank you" and "please," simple acts such as opening doors or holding a chair can go a long way in demonstrating respect toward each other. As the years go by, so many couples no longer display common courtesies, but take each other for granted, going from a servant's heart to a demanding heart. Your offspring learn their good manners (or bad ones) by watching how you treat each other.

• Laugh Together Daily—The Holy Bible says laughter is "good medicine." Tell each other funny stories, swap humorous cards and cartoons. The famous actress Ethel Barrymore said, "You finally grow up the day you can have your first good laugh at yourself." Don't take yourself so seriously. That helps create a healthy, healing atmosphere in a family.

• Speak Highly of Your Mate to Your Kids—Say things like: "You have a great mom, and I have a great wife," or, "Look at the super job your dad did in the yard." Faithfully build each other up. Since children are imitators, they will learn to show respect and build others up if they have watched you do the same.

• Watch Your Tone of Voice—It isn't always what you say, but how you say it that makes the difference. We need to be sure our tone shows patience and kindness toward others. The way you talk to each other is preparing those ankle biters in your house for the day they have mates of their own.

• Readily Forgive—Like we said at the beginning, we oftentimes don't do or say things we should or do and say things we shouldn't. Because of this, the two of us have a spirit of forgiveness in our home. What that means is that when one of us "blows it," the other one extends forgiveness. That also means the one "blowing it" admits it. Making a mistake isn't fatal. It gives you room to grow without being fearful that you have to do everything perfect.

By doing these things, husbands and wives are practicing Ephesians 4:32: "Be kind and compassionate to one another, forgiving each other, just as in Christ, God forgave you."

(Used by permission of Bob and Yvonne Turnbull, authors, speakers and life coaches. www.turnbullministries.org)

How to Know Whether or Not You Are Ready to Have Children

This could also go for grandparents who might think of having the little dears over for a week or so!

MESS TEST—Smear peanut butter on the sofa and curtains. Place a fish stick behind the couch and leave it there all summer.

TOY TEST—Obtain a 55-gallon box of Legos (or you may substitute roofing tacks), and have a friend spread them all over the house. Put on a blindfold. Try to walk to the bathroom or the kitchen. Do not scream because this would wake a child at night.

GROCERY STORE TEST—Borrow one or two small animals (goats are best) and take them shopping with you. Always keep them in sight, and pay for anything they eat or damage.

DRESSING TEST—Obtain one large, unhappy octopus. Stuff it into a small net bag, making sure all the arms stay inside.

ARE YOU BEGINNING TO WONDER?

FEEDING TEST—Obtain a large, plastic milk jug. Fill it halfway with water and suspend it from the ceiling with a cord. Now start the jug swinging and try to insert spoonfuls of soggy cereal into the mouth of the jug while pretending to be on an airplane. Then dump the contents of the jug on the floor.

NIGHT TEST—Prepare by obtaining a small cloth bag and filling it with eight to twelve pounds of sand. Soak it thoroughly in water. At 3 p.m., begin to waltz and hum with the bag until 9 p.m. Lay down the bag and set your alarm for 10 p.m. Get up, pick it up again, and sing every song you have ever heard. Make up about a dozen more songs and sing these too until 4 a.m. Set your alarm for 5 a.m. Get up and make breakfast. Keep this up for five years, while trying to look cheerful.

INGENUITY TEST—Take an egg carton. Using a pair of scissors and a can of paint, turn it into an alligator. Now take a toilet paper tube and turn it into an attractive Christmas candle using only scotch tape and a piece of foil. Last, take a milk carton, a ping-pong ball, and an empty box of Cocoa Puffs. Make an exact replica of the Eiffel Tower. Good Luck!

AUTOMOBILE TEST—Forget the BMW and buy a station wagon. Buy a chocolate ice cream cone and put it in the glove compartment. Leave it there. Get a dime and stick it into the cassette player. Now mash a family-size package of chocolate chip cookies into the back seat. There, perfect.

PHYSICAL TEST (women)—Obtain a large beanbag chair and attach it to the front of your clothes. Leave it there for nine months. Now remove ten of the beans.

PHYSICAL TEST (men)—Go to the nearest drug store. Set your wallet on the counter. Ask the clerk to help himself. Now proceed to the food store. Go to the head office and arrange for your paycheck to be directly deposited into the store. Purchase a newspaper and go home and read it quietly for the last time.

FINAL ASSIGNMENT—Find a couple that already has a small child. Lecture them on how they can improve discipline, patience, tolerance, toilet training, and their child's table manners. Suggest many ways they can improve. Emphasize to them that their children should never be allowed to run wild. Enjoy this experience, for it will be the last time you will have all the answers.

The Love Dress

The mother-in-law stopped by unexpectedly at the recently married couple's house. She rang the doorbell and stepped into the house. She saw her daughter-in-law standing naked by the door. "What are you doing?" she asked.

"I'm waiting for your son to come home from work," the daughter-in-law answered.

"But you're naked!" the mother-in-law exclaimed.

"This is my love dress," the daughter-in-law explained.

"Love dress? But you're naked!"

"Your son loves me to wear this dress! It makes him happy, and it makes me happy. I would appreciate it if you would leave because he will be home from work any minute."

The mother-in-law was tired of all this romantic talk, so she left. On the way home, she thought about the love dress and her own husband.

When she got home, she undressed, showered, put on her best perfume, and waited by the front door.

Finally, her husband came home. He walked in and saw her standing naked by the door. "What are you doing?" he asked.

"This is my love dress," she replied.

"Needs ironing!"

Kid Talk

What Does Love Mean?

A group of professional people posed this question to a group of 4 to 8-year-olds, "What does love mean?" The answers they got were broader and deeper than anyone could have imagined. See what you think:

"When my grandmother got arthritis, she couldn't bend over and paint her toenails anymore. So, my grandfather does it for her all the time, even when his hands got arthritis too. That's love." — Rebecca, age 8

"When someone loves you, the way they say your name is different. You know that your name is safe in their mouth." — Billy, age 4

"Love is when a girl puts on perfume, a boy puts on shaving cologne, and they go out and smell each other." — Karl, age 5

"Love is when you go out to eat and give somebody most of your French fries without making them give you any of theirs." — Chrissy, age 6

"Love is what makes you smile when you're tired." — Terri, age 4

"Love is when my mommy makes coffee for my daddy and she takes a sip before giving it to him, to make sure the taste is OK." — Danny, age 7

"Love is what's in the room with you at Christmas if you stop opening presents and listen." — Bobby, age 5

"If you want to learn to love better, you should start with a friend that you hate." — Nikka, age 6

"There are two kinds of love. Our love. God's love. But God makes both kinds of them." — Jenny, age 4

"Love is when you tell a guy you like his shirt, then he wears it every day." — Noelle, age 7

"Love is like a little old woman and a little old man who are still friends even after they know each other real good." —Tommy, age 6

"My mommy loves me more than anybody. You don't see anyone else kissing me to sleep at night." —Clare, age 5

"Love is when Mommy gives Daddy the best piece of chicken." —Elaine, age 5

"Love is when Mommy sees Daddy smelly and sweaty and still says he is handsomer than Robert Redford." —Chris, age 8

"Love is when your puppy licks your face even after you left him alone all day." —Mary Ann, age 4

"I know my older sister loves me because she gives me all her old clothes and has to go out and buy new ones." —Lauren, age 4

"I let my big sister pick on me because my Mom says she only picks on me because she loves me. So I pick on my baby sister because I love her." —Bethany, age 4

"When you love somebody, your eyelashes go up and down and little stars come out of you." —Karen, age 7

"Love is when Mommy sees Daddy on the toilet and she doesn't think it's gross." —Mark, age 6

"You really shouldn't say 'I love you' unless you mean it. But if you mean it, you should say it a lot. People forget." —Jessica, age 8

Goldfish

Little Tim was in the garden filling a hole when his neighbor peered over the fence. Interested in what the cheeky-faced youngster was up to, he politely asked, "What are you up to there, Tim?"

"My goldfish died," replied Tim tearfully without looking up, "and I've just buried him?"

The neighbor was concerned. "That's an awfully big hole for a goldfish, isn't it?"

Tim patted down the last heap of earth, then replied, "That's because he's inside your stupid cat!"

Freckles

An elderly woman and her little grandson, whose face was sprinkled with many freckles, spent the day at the zoo. Lots of children were waiting in line to get their cheeks painted by a local artist who was decorating them with tiger paws.

"You've got so many freckles, there's no place to paint!" a girl in the line said to the little fella.

Embarrassed, the little boy dropped his head.

His grandmother knelt down next to him. "I love your freckles. When I was a little girl, I always wanted freckles," she said while tracing her finger across the child's cheek. "Freckles are beautiful!"

The boy looked up, "Really?"

"Of course," said the grandmother. "Why, just name me one thing that's more beautiful than freckles."

The little boy thought for a moment, peered intensely into his grandma's face, and softly whispered, "Wrinkles."

Family Planning

A six-year-old boy told his father he wanted to marry the little girl across the street. The father, being modern and well-schooled in handling children, hid his smile behind his hand. "That's a serious step," he said. "Have you thought it out completely?"

"Sure," his young son answered. "We can spend one week in my room and the next in hers. It's right across the street, so I can run home if I get lonely in the night."

"How about transportation?" the father asked.

"I have my wagon, and we both have our tricycles," the little boy answered. The boy had an answer to every question the father raised.

Finally, in exasperation, the man asked, "What about babies? When you're married, you're liable to have babies, you know."

"We've thought about that, too," the little boy replied. "We're not going to have babies. Every time she lays an egg, I'm going to step on it."

Son, Get a Haircut

A young boy had just gotten his driving permit. He asked his father, who was a minister, if they could discuss the use of the car.

Taking father took him to his study, the father said to him, "I'll make a deal with you. Bring your grades up, study your Bible a little, get your hair cut, and we'll talk about it."

After about a month, the boy came back asking his father if they could further discuss use of the car. They again went to the father's study where his father said, "Son, I'm real proud of you. You have brought your grades up, and studied your Bible diligently, but you didn't get your hair cut!"

The young man waited a moment and replied, "You know Dad, I've been thinking about that. You know, Samson had long hair,

Moses had long hair, Noah had long hair, and even Jesus had long hair …"

To which his father replied, "Yes, and they WALKED everywhere they went!"

Kids Advice to Kids

"Never trust a dog to watch your food." Patrick, age 10

"When your dad is mad and asks you, 'Do I look stupid?' don't answer." Hannah, 9

"Never tell your mom her diet's not working." Michael, 14

"Stay away from prunes." Randy, 9

"Never pee on an electric fence." Robert, 13

"Don't squat with your spurs on." Noronha, 13

"Don't pull Dad's finger when he tells you to." Emily, 10

"When your mom is mad at your dad, don't let her brush your hair." Taylia, 11

"Never allow your three-year-old brother in the same room as your school assignment." Traci, 14

"Don't sneeze in front of mom when you're eating crackers." Mitchell, 12

"Puppies still have bad breath even after eating a Tic-Tac." Andrew, 9

"Never hold a dust buster and a cat at the same time." Kyoyo, 9

"You can't hide a piece of broccoli in a glass of milk." Armir, 9

"Don't wear polka-dot underwear under white shorts." Kellie, 11

"If you want a kitten, start out asking for a horse." Naomi, 15

"Felt markers are not good to use as lipstick." Lauren, 9

"Don't pick on your sister when she's holding a baseball bat." Joel, 10

"When you get a bad grade in school, show it to your mom when she's on the phone. Alyesha, 13

"Never try to baptize a cat." Eileen, 8

My Dad Is Better Than Yours

Three boys in school were bragging about their fathers. The first boy said, "My Dad scribbles a few words on a piece of paper. He calls it a poem, and they give him $50."

The second boy said, "That's nothing. My Dad scribbles a few words on a piece of paper. He calls it a song, and they give him $100."

The third boy said, "I got you both beat. My Dad scribbles a few words on a piece of paper. He calls it a sermon, and it takes eight people to collect all the money!"

The Cyberspace Classroom

Schoolroom Proverbs

A first-grade teacher collected well-known proverbs. She gave each child in her class the first half of a proverb and asked them to come up with the remainder of the proverb. It's hard to believe these were actually done by first-graders, but there are some good ones. The insights may surprise you.

Better to be safe than … … … … … … punch a 5th grader.
Strike while the … … … … … … … bug is close.
It's always the darkest before … … … Daylight Savings Time.
Never underestimate the power of … … …termites.
You can lead a horse to water but … … … how?
Don't bite the hand that … … … … … looks dirty.
No news is … … … … … … … … … impossible.
A miss is as good as a … … … … … … Mr.

You can't teach an old dog new ... ... math.

If you lie down with dogs, you'll ... ... stink in the morning.

Love all, trust ... ... me.

The pen is mightier than the ... ... pigs.

An idle mind is ... ... the best way to relax.

Where there's smoke there's ... ... pollution.

Happy is the bride who ... ... gets all the presents.

A penny saved is ... ... not much.

Two's company, three's ... ... .the Musketeers.

Don't put off till tomorrow what ... ... you put on to go to bed.

Laugh and the whole word laughs with you, cry and ... ...
... ... you have to blow your nose.

Children should be seen and not ... ... spanked or grounded.

If at first you don't succeed ... ... get new batteries.

You get out of something only what you ... ... see in the
picture on the box.

When the blind leadeth the blind ... ... get out of the way.

And the favorite: Better late than ... ... pregnant.

The Blue Ribbon

A teacher in New York decided to honor each of her seniors in high school by telling them the difference each made. She called each student to the front of the class, one at a time. First she told each of them how they had made a difference to her and the class. Then she presented each of them with a blue ribbon imprinted with gold letters, which read, "Who I Am Makes a Difference."

Afterwards, the teacher decided to do a class project to see what kind of impact "recognition" would have on a community. She gave each of the students three more ribbons and instructed them to go out and spread this acknowledgment ceremony. Then they were to follow up on the results, see who honored whom, and report back to the class in about a week.

One of the boys in the class honored a junior executive in a nearby company for helping with his career planning. The boy pinned a blue ribbon on his shirt. Then he gave him two extra ribbons and said, "We're doing a class project on recognition. We'd like you to go out, find somebody to honor, give them a blue ribbon, then give them the extra blue ribbon so they can acknowledge a third person to keep this acknowledgment ceremony going. Then please report back to me and tell what happened."

Later that day the junior executive went in to see his boss, who, by the way, had been noted as being kind of a grouchy fellow. He sat his boss down and told him that he deeply admired his creative genius. The boss seemed very surprised. The junior executive asked if he would accept the gift of the blue ribbon and for permission to pin it on him?

His surprised boss said, "Well, sure."

The junior executive placed the blue ribbon right on his boss's jacket right above his heart. As he gave him the last extra ribbon, he said, "Would you do me a favor? Would you take this extra one and pass it on by honoring somebody else? The young boy who first gave me the ribbons is doing a project in school and we want to keep this recognition ceremony going to find out how it affects people."

That night the boss came home to his 14-year-old son and sat him down. He said, "The most incredible thing happened to me today. I was in my office and one of the junior executives came in and told me he admired me. He gave me a blue ribbon for being a creative genius. Imagine, he thinks I'm a creative genius.

"Then he put this blue ribbon that says 'Who I Am Makes a Difference' on my jacket above my heart. He gave me an extra ribbon and asked me to find somebody else to honor. As I was driving home tonight, I started thinking about who to honor with this ribbon and I thought about you. I want to honor you. My days are really hectic, and when I come home, I don't pay a lot of attention to you. Sometimes I scream at you for not getting good enough grades in school or for your bedroom being a mess. But somehow, tonight, I just wanted to sit here and, well, just let you know that you do make a difference to me. Besides your mother, you are the most important person in my life. You're a great kid and I love you!"

The startled boy started to sob and sob, and he wouldn't stop crying. His whole body shook. He looked up at his father and said through his tears, "Dad, earlier tonight I sat in my room and wrote a letter to you and Mom explaining why I had killed myself and asking you to forgive me. I was going to commit suicide tonight after you were asleep. I just didn't think that you cared at all. The letter is upstairs. I don't think I need it after all."

His father walked upstairs and found a heartfelt letter full of anguish and pain. The envelope was addressed, "Mom and Dad."

The boss went back to work a changed man. He was no longer a grouch but made sure to let all his employees know that they made a difference.

The junior executive helped several other young people with career planning and never forgot to let them know that they made a difference in his life. One of these was the boss's son. The young boy and his classmates learned a valuable lesson, that who you are *does* make a difference.

Wisdom from Student Writings

This comes from a Catholic elementary school. Kids were asked questions about the Old and New Testaments. They have not been retouched or corrected (incorrect spelling has been left in.) Enjoy!

• In the first book of the Bible, Guinessis, God got tired of creating the world, so he took the Sabbath off.

• Adam and Eve were created from an apple tree. Noah's wife was called Joan of Ark. Noah built an ark, which the animals come on to in pears.

• Lot's wife was a pillar of salt by day, but a ball of fire by night.

• The Jews were a proud people and throughout history, they had trouble with the unsympathetic Genitals.

• Samson was a strong man who let himself be led astray by a Jezebel like Delilah.

• Moses led the Hebrews to the Red Sea, where they made unleavened bread, which is bread without any ingredients.

• The Egyptians were all drowned in the dessert. Afterwards, Moses went up on Mount Cyanide to get the ten amendments.

• The seventh commandment is thou shalt not admit adultery.

• Moses died before he ever reached Canada. Then Joshua led the Hebrews in the battle of Geritol.

• The greatest miracle in the Bible is when Joshua told his son to stand still and he obeyed him.

• David was a Hebrew king skilled at playing the liar. He fought with the Finklesteins, a race of people who lived in Biblical times.

• Solomon, one of David's sons, had 300 wives and 700 porcupines.

• When Mary heard that she was the mother of Jesus, she sang the Magna Carta.

• When the three wise guys from the east side arrived, they found Jesus in the manager.

• Jesus was born because Mary had an immaculate contraption.

• Jesus enunciated the Golden Rule, which says to do one to others before they do one to you. He also explained, "a man doth not live by sweat alone."

• It was a miracle when Jesus rose from the dead and managed to get the tombstone off the entrance.

• The people who followed the lord were called the 12 decibels. The epistles were the wives of the apostles.

• One of the opossums was St. Matthew who was also a taxi man.

• St. Paul cavorted to Christianity. He preached holy acrimony, which is another name for marriage.

• Christians have only one spouse. This is called monotony.

The Family Pet

Dear Buddy

You changed our world during the past ten years. You were such a good, kind, gentle dog. You protected us, kept away the raccoons, let the deer and birds play around our house. You never did catch the red fox or the rabbits. They were always too fast for you.

You watched the driveway from the deck. You ran around the deck checking that everything was okay. You wandered every inch of Spyglass Ridge. It was your home. You raced down the driveway to meet us every day and raced us back to the house, always beating us.

You were as white as the snow ... and sometimes we couldn't find you in the snow. Your white little ears popped up when we talked to you. You were so smart, we often had to spell words that we knew would excite you—like play, ride, walk.

And when we did take you for a walk, you went crazy with excitement. You pulled us down the hill to the lake where you raced into the water for a cool dip. And then with your pulling ability, made our walk up the hill much easier.

You loved everyone—kids, adults, and most of all us. We rewarded you with treats for your love, your obedience, and your many playful tricks. We're going to miss you, Buddy, because we loved you so much.

But here in your final resting place overlooking the fields and mountains, you can still watch over the property, and most of all over us. You can dream of chasing that red fox through the buffalo grass. And every time we see him, we'll always think of you.

"Thank You, God, for such a nice faithful companion, and guide us in the Spirit to the next dog you want to carry on where Buddy left off."

God bless you, Buddy.

Mom and Dad

(Dave Balsiger's eulogy to his American Eskimo dog.)

Leaving a Legacy

A Wise Investment

Are you aware that if we died tomorrow, the company that we are working for could easily replace us in a matter of days? But the family we left behind will feel the loss for the rest of their lives. And come to think of it, we pour ourselves into our work more than into our family—an unwise investment indeed, don't you think? So, what is behind the story?

Do you know what the word FAMILY means?

FAMILY = (F)ATHER (A)ND (M)OTHER (I) (L)OVE (Y)OU.

I Wish You Enough

Recently, at an airport, I overheard a father and daughter in their last moments together. Her flight's departure had been announced, and they were standing near the security gate. They hugged each other and he said, "I love you. I wish you enough."

She in turn said, "Daddy, our life together has been more than enough. Your love is all I ever needed. I wish you enough, too, Daddy."

They kissed and she left. He walked over toward the window where I was seated. Standing there, I could see he wanted and needed to cry. I tried not to intrude on his privacy, but he welcomed me in by asking, "Did you ever say good-bye to someone knowing it would be forever?"

"Yes, I have," I replied. Saying that brought back memories I had of expressing my love and appreciation for all my Dad had done for me. Recognizing that his days were limited, I took the time to tell him face to face how much he meant to me. So I knew what this man was experiencing.

"Forgive me for asking, but why is this a forever good-bye?" I asked.

"I am old and she lives much too far away. I have challenges ahead and the reality is, her next trip back will be for my funeral," he said.

"When you were saying good-bye, I heard you say, 'I wish you enough.' May I ask what that means?"

He began to smile. "That's a wish that has been handed down from other generations. My parents used to say it to everyone." He paused for a moment, looking up as if trying to remember it in detail. He smiled even more.

"When we said, 'I wish you enough,' we were wishing for the other person a life filled with just enough good things to sustain them," he continued. Turning toward me, he shared the following as if he were reciting it from memory.

"I wish you enough sun to keep your attitude bright.

I wish you enough rain to appreciate the sun more.

I wish you enough happiness to keep your spirit alive.

I wish you enough pain so that the smallest joys in life appear much bigger.

I wish you enough gain to satisfy your wanting.

I wish you enough loss to appreciate all that you possess.

I wish you enough Hello's to get you through the final Good-bye."

He then began to sob and walked away.

Friends, I wish you enough …

She's PC; He's Mac: The Gender Gap

4

Recognizing Our Differences

The South Pole

Why Women Cry

Top 10 Reasons Eve Was Created

How to Recognize a Good Woman

The Heart of a Woman

The North Pole

God Is Looking for Men Who Are ...

Get a Dog!

Broomdom

Why Men Are (Justifiably) Proud of Themselves

Recognizing Our Differences

What first reactions do you have to these events?

• The death of a family member. Do you cry or do you hold it all in?

• Spilled milk. Do you run for a paper towel or do you stand and look at the mess with your hands on your hips?

• News that there's nothing available in the kitchen for the next family meal. Do you rummage through the cupboards looking for something or grab the telephone to dial the pizza delivery person?

Our reactions to events don't always fit into stereotypical patterns, but generally, men react differently than women. That's what makes this world so interesting. Men will never completely understand women; women will never completely understand men. Men live at the North Pole and women at the South Pole. They can see each other over the equator—but just barely.

What problems have you encountered because you can't understand someone of the opposite sex? We've all had those run-ins where we shook our heads and said, "I just don't understand (wo)men!"

If you have children of the opposite sex, you are even more deeply mired in the differences between the sexes. A father shakes his head when his daughter bursts into tears over a minor issue. A mother frowns when her son throws his shoe and breaks a china vase in the living room. We're so different that it almost feels like we're incompatible—a PC and a Mac. What do we do when we find ourselves facing these differences?

We celebrate our differences by enjoying each other. That's what these entries do in this section of the book. They celebrate the quirks and oddities of each sex.

The South Pole

Why Women Cry

A little boy asked his mother, "Why are you crying?"

"Because I'm a woman," she told him.

"I don't understand," he said.

His mom just hugged him and said, "And you never will."

Later the little boy asked his father, "Why does mother seem to cry for no reason?"

"All women cry for no reason," was all his dad could say.

The little boy grew up and became a man, still wondering why women cry.

Finally, he put in a call to God. When God got on the phone, he asked, "God, why do women cry so easily?"

God said, "When I made the woman, she had to be special.

I made her shoulders strong enough to carry the weight of the world, yet gentle enough to give comfort.

I gave her an inner strength to endure childbirth and the rejection that many times comes from her children.

I gave her a hardness that allows her to keep going when everyone else gives up, and caring for her family through sickness and fatigue without complaining.

I gave her the sensitivity to love her children under any and all circumstances, even when the child has hurt her very badly.

I gave her strength to carry her husband through his faults and fashioned her from his rib to protect his heart.

I gave her wisdom to know that a good husband never hurts his wife, but sometimes tests her strengths and resolve to stand beside him unfalteringly.

And finally, I gave her a tear to shed. This is hers exclusively to use whenever it is needed."

"You see, my son," said God, "the beauty of a woman is not in the clothes she wears, the figure that she carries, or the way she combs her hair.

The beauty of a woman must be seen in her eyes, because that is the doorway to her heart—the place where love resides."

Top 10 Reasons Eve Was Created

10. God decided that Adam had too many ribs.

9. God knew that Adam would never go out and get a new fig leaf when the old one wore out.

8. God knew that Adam would never wash the dishes or vacuum the rug.

7. God knew that Adam would never remember to take out the garbage.

6. God knew that Adam would neglect to feed the dog.

5. God knew that if the world was only populated by men, they would all die of malnutrition.

4. God knew that, as keeper of the garden, Adam would never remember to cut the grass.

3. God knew that if there were only men, who would they blame?

2. As Genesis 2:18 says, "The Lord God said: 'It is not good for man to be alone' ... "

But, the number *one* reason that God created Eve ...

1. When God had finished creating Adam, He stepped back, scratched His head, and exclaimed, "I *know* that I can do better than that!"

How to Recognize a Good Woman

A good woman is proud. She respects herself and others. She is aware of who she is. She neither seeks definition from the person she is with, nor does she expect him to read her mind. She is quite capable of articulating her needs.

A good woman is hopeful. She is strong enough to make all her dreams come true. She knows love, therefore she gives love. She recognizes that her love has great value and must be reciprocated. If her love is taken for granted, it soon disappears.

A good woman has a dash of inspiration and a dabble of endurance. She knows that she will at times have to inspire others to reach the potential God gave them. A good woman knows her past, understands her present, and faces toward the future.

A good woman knows God. She knows that with God, the world is her playground, but without God, she will just be played with.

A good woman does not live in fear of the future because of her past. Instead, she understands that her life experiences are merely lessons meant to bring her closer to self-knowledge and unconditional self-love.

The Heart of a Woman

By the time the Lord made woman, He was into his sixth day and working overtime. An angel appeared and said, "Why are you spending so much time on this one?"

The Lord answered, "Have you seen the spec sheet on her? She has to be completely washable, but not plastic, have 200 movable parts, all replaceable, run on black coffee and leftovers, have a lap that can hold two children at one time and disappears when she stands up, have a kiss that can cure anything from a scraped knee to a broken heart, and have six pairs of hands."

The angel was astounded at the requirements for this one. "Six pairs of hands! No way!"

The Lord replied, "Oh, it's not the hands that are the problem. It's the three pairs of eyes that mothers must have!"

"And that's just on the standard model?" the angel asked.

The Lord nodded. "Yep, one pair of eyes is to see through the closed doors as she asks her children what they are doing even though she already knows. Another pair in the back of her head is to see what she needs to know even though no one thinks she can. And the third pair is here in the front of her head. They are for looking at an errant child and conveying that she understands and loves him or her without even saying a single word."

The angel tried to stop the Lord. "This is too much work for one day. Wait until tomorrow to finish."

"But I can't!" the Lord protested. "I am so close to finishing this creation that is so dear to my own heart. She already heals herself when she is sick *and* can feed a family on a pound of hamburger and can get a nine year old to stand in the shower."

The angel moved closer and touched the woman, "But you have made her so soft, Lord,"

"She is soft," the Lord agreed, "but I have also made her tough. You have no idea what she can endure or accomplish."

"Will she be able to think?" asked the angel.

The Lord replied, "Not only will she be able to think, she will be able to reason and negotiate."

The angel then noticed something, reached out, and touched the woman's cheek. "Oops, it looks like this model has a leak. I told you that you were trying to put too much into this one."

"That's not a leak," the Lord objected. "That's a tear!"

"What's the tear for?" the angel asked.

The Lord said, "The tear is her way of expressing her joy, her sorrow, her pain, her disappointment, her loneliness, her grief, and her pride."

The angel was impressed. "Lord, you thought of everything, for women are truly amazing."

Women have strengths that amaze men. They carry children; they carry hardships; they carry burdens; but they hold happiness, love, and joy. They smile when they want to scream. They sing when they want to cry. They cry when they are happy and laugh when they are nervous. They fight for what they believe in. They stand up for injustice. They don't take "no" for an answer when they believe there is a better solution. They go without new shoes so their children can have them. They go to the doctor with a frightened friend.

They love unconditionally. They cry when their children excel and cheer when their friends get awards. Their hearts break when a friend dies. They have sorrow at the loss of a family member, yet they are strong when they think there is no strength left. They know that a hug and a kiss can heal a broken heart.

Women come in all sizes, in all colors and shapes. They'll drive, fly, walk, run, or e-mail you to show how much they care about you. The heart of a woman is what makes the world spin! Women do more than give birth. They bring joy and hope. They give compassion and ideals. Women have a lot to say and a lot to give.

The North Pole

God Is Looking for Men Who Are …

Men who are Authentic and men who are Available!

Authentic

First Thessalonians 2:12 says, "We are to live lives worthy of God." This is lived out in your everyday life. Your wife, children, coworkers, and friends have video-camera eyes and audiotape-recording ears. They see and hear *everything*. Authentic means you are the same on the outside as you are on the inside. There are many ways to be authentic. Here are two of them:

1. Walk Your Talk

An authentic man wouldn't state, "I'm a Christian," and then act in a way that belies that statement. An example: When a man tells his children not to tell lies but then gets a phone call at home from someone he doesn't want to talk to, so he whispers to one of his kids, "Tell them I'm not in and won't be back for three days."

Or he peaceably attends church service, but when he comes home, he uses anger to get his way with a family member. Is that walking the talk? At work he wears a WWJD (What Would Jesus Do) bracelet, and then goes home with some stolen office supplies. Or, what do you think his coworkers think about him when he laughs at dirty jokes right after telling them about the church revival he attended the night before? Our actions set an example for how our kids, our spouse, and our coworkers view God.

We should strive to be authentic, but when we fall short, we should also be willing to admit when we've blown it. Our loved ones already know we've blown it. Hey, they live with us, and it's not hard to spot. We need to apologize to them and ask for their forgiveness. We're teaching them that when they make a mistake, it's not the end of their world. They can admit it and grow from it.

2. Keep Your Promises

If you promise your kids or spouse something, *keep your promise*. Be consistent. The number one resentment with kids comes from the broken promises of their parents. To a child, "probably, perhaps, or maybe" means yes. Only mention aloud what you can follow through.

One of the biggest areas in which we often disappoint our family is with our time schedule. To enable you to keep your promises, make your appointments with loved ones nonnegotiable commitments. Put them on your calendar first, and then schedule other things around them. By doing that, your family learns to trust that you're a man of your word, otherwise, you won't spend the quality time with them you should. You don't want to end your life full of family regrets.

Available

A man needs to be available to his family and God. Here are two ways to do that:

1. To Family

Too often, as men we focus on being a success at work, and then aren't available with our time and energy for our wife and our children. Or when we are with them, we sometimes make them feel like we can only spend time with them during the commercials. The message we're giving them is that they aren't a priority—and truthfully, they're not.

I am aware this is a constant balancing act for us. For too many years, I didn't balance it well and made my family feel that they were infringing on my time frames, that I had more important things to do. Fortunately, God woke me up before I lost everything. Here are a few things I implemented into my life.

• Live in the now. When you spend time with the family, "be there." That means not just physically being there, but also emotionally. Actually, be involved in whatever you're doing and not focused on what you think you'd rather be doing.

• Plan regularly scheduled family nights. They could be once-a-week fun nights where each family member gets his turn to pick what the family will do that night.

• Date your mate on a regular basis. You need to have face-to-face time with one another. It's a special time to have fun and stay connected. It helps, too, if you do the planning and get the babysitter.

- Date your children—one child at a time, an exclusive time with dad—hiking, going to the zoo or park, getting ice cream. Make sure it's a time when you can talk. When your child knows he can have your full attention, he will often share his deepest thoughts with you.
- Daily practice good listening. To get your family to talk to you, make sure they know that you're willing to listen to them. To be a better listener, get rid of distractions. Turn off the TV and get away from the computer so you can focus on the person and the conversation you're going to have. Listen without interrupting or changing the subject and maintain eye contact. Eye contact sends a powerful message to them that what they're saying is important. Plus it also lets you watch their body language, which tells you what they're really trying to say.

2. To God

Are you willing to be used daily by God to make a difference in the lives of others? God wants available men who have a heart full of trust and faith, and will be obedient to what God shows them—especially in our families where God has called us to be the spiritual leaders. A couple of suggestions on how to make this a reality:

- Lead your family into a vital relationship with Jesus Christ. This needs to be our #1 priority. Since more things are "caught not taught," model this by having a growing daily relationship with Jesus Christ (Matthew 22:37). Take time to study the Bible to better know God and His will. Through the Word of God and talking with God in prayer, God works on the inner man so that we can become men after God's own heart. As your family sees you growing and changing, they will better understand what a relationship with our Lord is all about.
- Pray for and with your wife and children. Lay your hands on your children. Bless them in the name of Jesus. Our family

implements the Three A's of Prayer; we all can pray Anytime, Anywhere, and about Anything.

• Lead family devotions. You can easily find lots of material in your local Christian bookstore. Two rules to remember for family devotions when children are participating: Keep them short and fun.

Men must walk the talk. Nothing more, nothing less, nothing else! Be all you can be for Christ, and watch Christ do all He can through you.

(Used by permission of Bob and Yvonne Turnbull, authors, speakers and
life coaches. www.turnbullministries.org)

Get a Dog!

If you want someone who will do anything to please you, get a dog.

If you want someone who will bring you the newspaper without tearing through it first for the sports page, get a dog.

If you want someone who'll make a total fool of himself because he's so glad to see you, get a dog.

If you want someone who eats whatever you put in front of him and never says his mother made it better, get a dog.

If you want someone who's always eager to go out any time you ask and anywhere you want to go, get a dog.

If you want someone who can scare away burglars without waving a lethal weapon around, endangering you and all the neighbors, get a dog.

If you want someone who never touches the remote, couldn't care less about Monday Night Football, and watches dramatic movies with you as long as you want, get a dog.

If you want someone who'll be content just to snuggle up and keep you warm in bed, and who you can kick out of bed if he slobbers and snores, get a dog.

If you want someone who never criticizes anything you do, doesn't care how good or bad you look, acts as though every word you say is worth hearing, never complains, and loves you unconditionally all the time, get a dog.

On the other hand ...

If you want someone who never comes when you call him, totally ignores you when you walk in the room, leaves hair all over the place, walks all over you, prowls around all night and comes home only to eat and sleep all day, and acts as though you are there only to see that HE's happy ...

Get a CAT!

Just realize that while men sometimes act like animals, we are both more independent and dependent than cats and dogs.

Broomdom

Two brooms were hanging in the closet. After a while, they got to know each other so well that they decided to get married. One broom was, of course, the bride broom. The other was the groom broom. The bride broom looked very beautiful in her white dress. The groom broom was handsome and suave in his tuxedo. The wedding was lovely. After the wedding, at the wedding dinner, the bride broom leaned over and said to the groom broom, "I think I am going to have a little whisk broom!!!"

"IMPOSSIBLE!!" said the groom broom.

Are you ready for this!!?

Scroll down ...

V

V

V

V

V

WE HAVEN'T EVEN SWEPT TOGETHER!!!

Why Men Are (Justifiably) Proud of Themselves

1. We know stuff about tanks.
2. A 5-day trip requires only one suitcase.
3. We can open all our own jars.
4. We can go to the bathroom without a support group.
5. We don't have to learn to spell a new last name.
6. We can leave a motel bed unmade.
7. We can kill our own food.
8. We get extra credit for the slightest act of thoughtfulness.
9. Wedding plans take care of themselves.
10. If someone forgets to invite us to something, he can still be our friend.
11. Underwear is $10 a three-pack.
12. If you are 34 and single, nobody notices.
13. Everything on our faces stays the original color.
14. We are always right.
15. We don't have to clean the house if the meter reader is coming.
16. Car mechanics tell us the truth.
17. We can sit quietly and watch a game with a friend for hours without thinking, "He must be mad at me."
18. Same work—more pay.
19. Gray hair and wrinkles only add character.
20. We can drop by and see a friend without having to bring a little gift.
21. If another guy shows up at a party in the same outfit, we just might become lifelong friends.
22. Our pals will never trap us with: "So, notice anything different?"
23. We are not expected to know the names of more than 5 colors.
24. We almost never have a "strap problem" in public.
25. We are totally unable to see wrinkles in our clothes.

26. The same hairstyle lasts for years—maybe decades.
27. We don't have to shave below the neck.
28. A few belches are expected and tolerated.
29. Our belly usually hides our big hips.
30. One wallet, one pair of shoes, one color, all seasons.
31. We can do our nails with a pocketknife.
32. We have freedom of choice concerning growing a mustache.
33. Christmas shopping can be accomplished for 25 people on the day before Christmas and in 45 minutes.

Click Here for Help

5

Help is On the Way

Tips for Healthy Living
The Best Gifts to Give
Instructions for Life
Always Read the Instructions
Coca-Cola Can Help and Hinder

Food for the Soul
Maybe ...
Truths to Guide the Soul
Emergency Phone Numbers
A to Z

Pointers from Nature
The "Honk" of Leadership
The Lesson of Geese

Virtual Priorities
How Do You Live Your Dash?
Wealth, Success, and Love

Passions for Life

Remember, Whatever Happens

Why the American Flag Is Folded

Only in America ...

Life's Issues

Daily Praise

Words from Jesus

True Values

That's God

Important Recall Notice

Help Is On the Way

You've had a hard day. Nothing's gone right, and you're at the end of your rope. Not knowing what to do with yourself, you sit down at the computer and log on to your e-mail address. All you see is spam and advertisements. But then, tucked away between the ads for prescription pills and home refinancing, you see one personal message from your close friend. You click on the message and up pops a poem. Amazingly, it addresses just the problem you're so discouraged about.

You eagerly read the words, and they act like a soothing balm to your soul. At the bottom of the poem, she has written a personal line or two to raise your spirits. They did just that! Your smile shows how much you appreciate your friend's thoughtfulness in sending you a cheery note.

You sit back and think of your other friends. Each one is struggling with some kind of difficulty in her life. One is going through a divorce. Another's youngest son just moved out, so she's dealing with the empty-nest syndrome. A third just had a baby—and she's well over forty!

You think, Where could I find a message that would help my friends with their life's' issues?

That's what this section is all about. Scan through the entries and find one that you know will encourage your friend. Or perhaps some are just the antidote you need for your own problems.

Here you will find entries from tips on how to beat fatigue, to locating Bible chapters for help in emergencies, to setting your priorities. Or you can find wisdom for your day. It's true. This is the place to "Click Here for Help."

Tips for Healthy Living

The Best Gifts to Give

The best gifts to give:
To your friend—loyalty
To your enemy—forgiveness
To your boss—service
To a child—a good example
To your parents—gratitude and devotion
To your mate—love and faithfulness
To all men and women—charity
To your God—your life

Instructions for Life

If you wish to have a contented life, practice these kernels of wisdom:
1. Give people more than they expect and do it cheerfully.
2. Memorize your favorite poem.
3. Don't believe all you hear, spend all you have, or sleep all you want.
4. When you say, "I love you," mean it.
5. When you say, "I'm sorry," look the person in the eye.
6. Be engaged at least six months before you get married.
7. Believe in love at first sight.
8. Never laugh at anyone's dreams.
9. Love deeply and passionately. You might get hurt, but it's the only way to live life completely.
10. In disagreements, fight fairly. No name calling.
11. Don't judge people by their relatives.

12. Talk slowly, but think quickly.

13. When someone asks you a question and you don't want to answer, smile, and ask, "Why do you want to know?"

14. Remember that great love and great achievements involve great risk.

15. Call your mom.

16. Say, "Bless you!" when you hear someone sneeze.

17. When you lose, don't lose the lesson.

18. Remember the three R's: Respect for self. Respect for others. Responsibility for all your actions.

19. Don't let a little dispute injure a great friendship.

20. When you realize you've made a mistake, take immediate steps to correct it.

21. Smile when picking up the phone. The caller will hear it in your voice.

22. Marry someone you love to talk to. As you get older, your mate's conversational skills will be as important as any other.

23. Spend some time alone.

24. Open your arms to change, but don't let go of your values.

25. Remember that silence is sometimes the best answer.

26. Read more books and watch less TV.

27. Live a good, honorable life. Then when you get older and think back, you'll enjoy it a second time.

28. Trust in God, but lock your car.

29. A loving atmosphere in your home is so important. Do all you can to create a tranquil, harmonious home.

30. In disagreements with loved ones, deal with the current situation. Don't bring up the past.

31. Read between the lines.

32. Share your knowledge. It's a way to achieve immortality.

33. Be gentle with the earth.

34. Pray. It has immeasurable power.

35. Never interrupt when you are being flattered.

36. Mind your own business.

37. Don't trust a man/woman who doesn't close his/her eyes when you kiss.

38. Once a year, go someplace you've never been before.

39. If you make a lot of money, put it to use helping others while you are living. That is wealth's greatest satisfaction.

40. Remember that not getting what you want is sometimes a blessing.

41. Learn the rules, and then break some.

42. Remember that the best relationship is one where your love for each other is greater than your need for each other.

43. Judge your success by what you had to give up to get it.

44. Remember that your character is your destiny.

45. Approach love and cooking with reckless abandon.

Always Read the Instructions

In case you needed further proof that the human race is doomed through stupidity, here are some actual label instructions on consumer goods.

On a Sear's hairdryer: Do not use while sleeping.

(*And that's the only time I have to work on my hair.*)

On a bag of Fritos: You could be a winner! No purchase necessary. Details inside.

(*The shoplifter special?*)

On a bar of Dial soap: "Directions: Use like regular soap."

(*And that would be how???*)

On some Swanson frozen dinners: "Serving suggestion: Defrost."

(*But, it's "just" a suggestion.*)

On Tesco's Tiramisu dessert (printed on bottom) "Do not turn upside down."

(*Well, duh, a bit late, huh?*)

On Marks and Spencer Bread Pudding: "Product will be hot after heating."

(*And you thought???*)

On packaging for a Rowenta iron: "Do not iron clothes on body."

(*But wouldn't this save me more time?*)

On Boot's Children Cough Medicine: "Do not drive a car or operate machinery after taking this medication.

(*We could do a lot to reduce the rate of construction accidents if we could just get those 5-year-olds with head colds off those forklifts.*)

On Nytol Sleep Aid: "Warning: May cause drowsiness."

(*And I'm taking this because???*)

On most brands of Christmas lights: "For indoor or outdoor use only."

(*As opposed to what?*)

On a Japanese food processor: "Not to be used for the other use."

(*Somebody out there, help me on this. I'm a bit curious.*)

On Sunsbury's peanuts: "Warning: contains nuts."

(*Talk about a news flash!*)

On an American Airlines packet of nuts: "Instructions: Open packet, eat nuts."

(*Step 3: maybe, uh, fly Delta?*)

On a child's Superman costume: Wearing of this garment does not enable you to fly."

(*I don't blame the company. I blame the parents for this one.*)

On a Swedish chainsaw: "Do not attempt to stop chain with your hands."

(*Was there a lot of this happening somewhere?*)

Coca-Cola Can Help and Hinder

Uses for Coca-Cola:

1. In many states in the USA, the highway patrol carries two gallons of Coca-Cola in the trunk to remove blood from the highway after a car accident.

2. You can put a T-bone steak in a bowl of Coca-Cola, and it will be gone in two days.

3. To clean a toilet: Pour a can of Coca-Cola into the toilet bowl and let the "real thing" sit for one hour, then flush clean. The citric acid in the Coca-Cola removes stains from vitreous china.

4. To remove rust spots from chrome car bumpers: Rub the bumper with a rumpled-up piece of Reynolds Wrap aluminum foil dipped in Coca-Cola.

5. To clean corrosion from car battery terminals: Pour a can of Coca-Cola over the terminal to bubble away the corrosion.

6. To loosen a rusted bolt: Apply a cloth soaked in Coca-Cola to the rusted bolt for several minutes.

7. To bake a moist ham: Empty a can of Coca-Cola into the baking pan. Wrap the ham in aluminum foil and bake. Thirty minutes before the ham is finished, remove the foil, and allow the drippings to mix with the Coca-Cola for a sumptuous brown gravy.

8. To remove grease from clothes: Empty a can of Coca-Cola into a load of greasy clothes, add detergent, and run through a regular cycle. The Coca-Cola will help to loosen grease stains.

9. Use Coca-Cola to clean road haze from your windshield.

Hazards of Coca-Cola:

1. The active ingredient in Coca-Cola is phosphoric acid, which among other things, leaches calcium from bones and is a major contributor to the rising increase in osteoporosis..

2. Coca-Cola will dissolve an iron nail in about 4 days.

3. To carry Coca-Cola syrup (the concentrate), commercial trucks must use the Hazardous Material placecards reserved for Highly Corrosive Materials.
4. The distributors of Coca-Cola have been using it to clean the engines of their trucks for about 20 years!

Food for the Soul

Maybe ...

Maybe ... God wanted us to meet the wrong people before meeting the right one so that when we finally meet the right person, we will know how to be grateful for that gift.

Maybe ... When the door of happiness closes, another opens. But often times we look so long at the closed door that we don't see the one that has been opened for us.

Maybe ... The best kind of friend is the kind you can sit on a porch and swing with, never saying a word, and then walk away feeling like it was the best conversation you've ever had.

Maybe ... It is true that we don't know what we have until we lose it. But it is also true that we don't know what we have been missing until it arrives.

Maybe ... Giving someone all your love is never an assurance that he or she will love you back. Don't expect love in return; just wait for it to grow in a heart, but if it does not, be content that it grew in yours.

Maybe … It takes only a minute to get a crush on someone, an hour to like someone, and a day to love someone, but it takes a lifetime to forget someone.

Maybe … You shouldn't go for looks; they can deceive. Don't go for wealth; even that fades away. Go for someone who makes you smile because it takes only a smile to make a dark day seem bright. Find the one that makes your heart smile.

Maybe … There are moments in life when you miss people so much that you just want to pluck them from your dreams and hug them for real.

Maybe … You should dream what you want to dream; go where you want to go; be what you want to be, because you have only one life and one chance to do all the things you want to do.

Maybe … You have enough happiness to make you sweet, enough trials to make you strong, enough sorrow to keep you human, and enough hope to make you happy.

Maybe … You should always put yourself in others' shoes. If you feel that it hurts you, it probably hurts the other person, too.

Maybe … The happiest of people don't necessarily have the best of everything; they just make the best of everything that comes along their way.

Maybe … Happiness lies for those who cry, those who hurt, those who have searched, and those who have tried, because only they can appreciate the importance of people who have touched their lives.

Maybe … Love begins with a smile, grows with a kiss, and ends with a tear.

Maybe … The brightest future will always be based on a forgotten past. You can't move on well in life until you let go of your past failures and heartaches.

Maybe … When you were born, you were crying and everyone around you was smiling. Live your life so that when you die, you are the one who is smiling and everyone around you is crying.

Truths to Guide the Soul

- Be fishers of men. You catch them—He'll clean them.
- Coincidence is when God chooses to remain anonymous.
- Don't insert a question mark where God has a period.
- Don't wait for six strong men to take you to church.
- Forbidden fruits create many jams.
- God doesn't call the qualified; He qualifies the called.
- God grades on the cross, not the curve.
- God loves everyone, but probably prefers "fruits of the spirit" over "religious nuts!"
- God promises a safe landing, not a calm passage.
- He, who angers you, controls you!
- If God is your copilot, swap seats!
- Most people want to serve God, but only in an advisory capacity.
- Prayer: Don't give God instructions, just report for duty!
- The task ahead of us is never as great as the Power behind us.
- The Will of God will never take you to where the Grace of God will not protect you.
- We don't change the message; the message changes us.

Emergency Phone Numbers

When in sorrow, ... call John 14.
When men fail you, ... call Psalm 27.
If you want to be fruitful, ... call John 15.
When you have sinned, ... call Psalm 51.
When you worry, ... call Matthew 6:19-34.
When you are in danger, ... call Psalm 91.
When God seems far away, ... call Psalm 139.
When your faith needs stirring, ... call Hebrews 11.
When you are lonely and fearful, ... call Psalm 23.
When you grow bitter and critical, ... call 1 Corinthians 13.
For Paul's secret to happiness, ...call Colossians 3:12-17.
For understanding of Christianity, ... call Corinthians 5:15-19.
When you feel down and out, ... call Romans 8:31.
When you want peace and rest, ... call Matthew 11:25-30.
When the world seems bigger than God, ... call Psalm 90.
When you want Christian assurance, ... call Romans 8:1-30.
When your prayers grow narrow or selfish, ... call Psalm 67.
For a great invention/opportunity, ... call Isaiah 55.
When you want courage for a task, ... call Joshua 1.
For how to get along with fellow men, ... call Romans 12.
When you think of investments and returns, ... call Mark 10.
If you are depressed, ... call Psalm 27.
If your pocketbook is empty,... call Psalm 37.
If you are losing confidence in people, ... call 1 Corinthians 13.
If people seem unkind, ... call John 15.
If discouraged about your work,... call Psalm 126.
If you find the world growing small and yourself great, ... call
Psalm 19.

Alternative numbers:
For dealing with fear, ... call Psalm 34:7.
For security, ... call Psalm 121:3.

For assurance, … call Mark 8:35.

For reassurance, … call Psalm 145:18

Emergency numbers can easily be found in any heavenly directory (Holy Bible), and its Author may be dialed direct. No operator assistance is necessary. All lines to Heaven are open 24 hours a day! Feed your faith, and doubt will starve to death!

A to Z

Whoever came up with this one must have had some divine guidance:

Although things are not perfect
Because of trial or pain,
Continue in thanksgiving;
Do not begin to blame.
Even when the times are hard
Fierce winds are bound to blow,
God is forever able.
Hold on to what you know.
Imagine life without His love;
Joy would cease to be.
Keep thanking Him for all the things
Love imparts to you.
Move out of "Camp Complaining."
No weapon that is known
On earth can yield the power
Praise can do alone.
Quit looking at the future;
Redeem the time at hand.
Start every day with worship.
To "thank" is a command.
Until we see Him coming

Victorious in the sky,
We'll run the race with gratitude
Xalting God most high.
Yes, there'll be good times and yes, some will be bad, but...
Zion waits in glory where none are ever sad.

The shortest distance between a problem and a solution is the distance between your knees and the floor. The one who kneels to the Lord can stand up to anything.
Love and peace be with you forever. Amen.

Pointers from Nature

The "Honk" of Leadership

"Obey your leaders and submit to their authority. They keep watch over you as men who must give an account. Obey them so that their work will be a joy, not a burden, for that would be of no advantage to you" (Hebrews 13:17, NIV).

Sandhill cranes provide a wonderful picture of teamwork. These large birds fly great distances due to some remarkable qualities. First, they rotate leadership so that no bird stays out in front all the time. Second, they only choose cranes that can lead the others through stiff winds and turbulence. With this type of bird in the lead, the rest will follow, honking their support and affirmation.

Want to be a better team player? Take a lesson from these cranes. They learn to support the one in the lead. Become a team player in your family, church, and neighborhood. Support the efforts of your leaders. Give a honk to those who need it.

The Lesson of the Geese

This fall, when you see geese heading south for the winter flying along in the "V" formation, you might consider what science has discovered as to why they fly that way.

Fact: As each bird flaps its wings, it creates an uplift for the bird immediately following. By flying in the "V" formation, the whole flock has at least 71 percent greater flying range than if each bird flew on its own.

Lesson: People who share a common direction and sense of community can get where they are going more quickly and easily because they are traveling on the thrust of one another.

Fact: When a goose flies out of formation, it suddenly feels the drag and resistance of trying to go it alone. It quickly gets back into formation to take advantage of the lifting power of the bird in front of it.

Lesson: If we have as much common sense as a goose, we stay in formation with those headed where we want to go. We are willing to accept their help and give our help to them. It is harder to do something alone than together.

Fact: When the lead goose gets tired, it rotates back into the formation and another goose flies to the point position.

Lesson: It is sensible to take turns doing the hard and demanding tasks and sharing leadership. As with geese, people are interdependent on each other's skills, capabilities, and unique possession of gifts, talents, or resources.

Fact: The geese flying in formation honk from behind to encourage those up front to keep up their speed.

Lesson: We need to make sure our honking is encouraging. In groups with encouragement, the production is much greater. The power of encouragement to stand by one's heart or core values and encourage the heart and core of others is the quality of honking we seek. We need to make sure our honking is encouraging and not discouraging.

Fact: When a goose gets sick, wounded, or shot down, two other geese will drop out of formation with that goose and follow it down to lend help and protection. They stay with the fallen goose until it dies or is able to fly again, then they launch out on their own or with another formation to catch up with their flock.

Lesson: If we have the sense of a goose, we will stand by our colleagues and each other in difficult times as well as in good times.

Bless you as we soar together.

"They overcame him by the blood of the lamb and the word of their testimony, not loving their lives even to death" (Revelation 12:11, NIV).

Virtual Priorities

How Do You Live Your Dash?

I read of a man who stood to speak
At the funeral of a friend.
He referred to the dates on her tombstone
From the beginning to the end.
He noted that first came her date of birth
And spoke the following date with tears,
But he said what mattered most of all
Was the dash between those years (1900-1970)
For that dash represents all the time
That she spent alive on earth ...
And now only those who loved her
Know what that little line is worth.
For it matters not how much we own—
The cars, the house, the cash—
What matters is how we live and love

And how we spend our dash.
So think about this long and hard …
Are there things you'd like to change?
For you never know how much time is left
That can still be rearranged.
If we could just slow down enough
To consider what's true and real,
And always try to understand
The way other people feel.
And be less quick to anger,
And show appreciation more
And love the people in our lives
Like we've never loved before.
If we treat each other with respect,
And more often wear a smile,
Remembering that this special dash
Might only last a little while.

Wealth, Success, and Love

A woman came out of her house and saw three old men with long white beards sitting in her front yard. She did not recognize them. She said, "I don't think I know you, but you must be hungry. Please come in and have something to eat."

"Is the man of the house home?" they asked.

"No," she replied. "He's out."

"Then we cannot come in," they replied.

In the evening when her husband came home, she told him what had happened.

"Go tell them I am home and invite them in!"

The woman went out and invited the men in.

"We do not go into a house together," they replied.

"Why is that?" she asked.

One of the old men explained, "His name is Wealth," he said pointing to one of his friends, then said pointing to another one, "He is Success, and I am Love." Then he added, "Now go in and discuss with your husband which one of us you want in your home."

The woman went in and told her husband what was said.

Her husband was overjoyed. "How nice!" he said. "Since that is the case, let us invite Wealth. Let him come and fill our home with wealth!"

His wife disagreed. "My dear, why don't we invite Success?"

Their daughter-in-law was listening from the other corner of the house. She jumped in with her own suggestion, "Would it not be better to invite Love? Our home will then be filled with love!"

"Let us heed our daughter-in-law's advice," said the husband to his wife. "Go out and invite Love to be our guest."

The women went out and asked the three old men, "Which one of you is Love? Please come in and be our guest."

Love got up and started walking toward the house. The other two got up and followed him. Surprised, the lady asked Wealth and Success, "I only invited Love, why are you coming in?"

The old men replied together, "If you had invited Wealth or Success, the other two of us would've stayed out, but since you invited Love, wherever he goes, we go with him. Wherever there is Love, there is also Wealth and Success!!!!!!"

Passions for Life

Remember, Whatever Happens

Read each one carefully and think about it a second or two.

1. I love you not because of who you are, but because of who I am when I am with you.

2. No man or woman is worth your tears, and the one who is, won't make you cry.

3. Just because someone doesn't love you the way you want them to doesn't mean he doesn't love you with all he has.

4. A true friend is someone who reaches for your hand and touches your heart.

5. The worst way to miss someone is to be sitting right beside him knowing you can't have him.

6. Never frown, even when you are sad, because you never know who is falling in love with your smile.

7. To the world, you may be one person, but to one person you may be the world.

8. Don't waste your time on a man/woman, who isn't willing to waste his/her time on you.

9. Maybe God wants us to meet a few wrong people before meeting the right one so that when we finally meet the person, we will know how to be grateful.

10. Don't cry because it is over; smile because it happened.

11. There are always going to be people who hurt you, so what you have to do is keep on trusting and just be more careful about who you trust next time around.

12. Make yourself a better person and know who you are before you try to know someone else, and expect him to know you.

13. Don't try so hard. The best things come when you least expect them to.

Remember: whatever happens, happens for a reason.

Why the American Flag is Folded 13 Times

Have you ever wondered why the flag of the United State of America is folded 13 times when it is lowered or when it is folded and handed to the next of kin at the burial of a veteran? Here is the meaning of each of those folds:

• The first fold of our flag is a symbol of life.
• The second fold is a symbol of our belief in eternal life.
• The third fold is made in honor and remembrance of the veterans departing our ranks who gave a portion of their lives for the defense of our country to attain peace throughout the world.
• The fourth fold represents our weaker nature. As American citizens, we must trust in times of peace as well as in time of war for God's divine guidance.
• The fifth fold is a tribute to our country. In the words of Stephen Decatur, "Our country, in dealing with other countries, may she always be right; but it is still our country, right or wrong."
• The sixth fold is for where our hearts lie. It is with our heart that we pledge allegiance to the flag of the United States of America, and to the Republic for which it stands, one nation under God, indivisible, with liberty and justice for all.
• The seventh fold is a tribute to our Armed Forces. It is through the Armed Forces that we protect our country and our flag against all her enemies, whether they are found within or without the boundaries of our Republic.
• The eighth fold is a tribute to the one who entered into the valley of the shadow of death that we might see the light of day and to honor mother, for whom it flies on Mother's Day.
• The ninth fold is a tribute to womanhood. It has been through their faith, love, loyalty, and devotion that the character of the men and women who have made this country great has been molded.
• The tenth fold is a tribute to the fathers. They, too, have given their sons and daughters for the defense of our country since they were first born.
• The eleventh fold, in the eyes of a Hebrew citizen, represents the lower portion of the seal of King David and King Solomon and glorifies the God of Abraham, Isaac, and Jacob.
• The twelfth fold, in the eyes of a Christian citizen, represents an emblem of eternity and glorifies God the Father, the Son, and Holy Spirit.

When the flag is completely folded, the stars are uppermost reminding us of our Nation's motto, "In God We Trust." After the flag is completely folded and tucked in, it takes on the appearance of a cocked hat, ever reminding us of the soldiers who served under General George Washington, and the Sailors and Marines who served under Captain John Paul Jones, who were followed by their comrades and shipmates in the Armed Forces of the United States, preserving for us the rights, privileges, and freedoms we enjoy today.

The next time you see a flag ceremony honoring someone who has served our country, either in the Armed Forces or in the civilian services such as the police force or fire departments, keep in mind all the important reasons behind each and every movement. They have paid the ultimate sacrifice for all of us by honoring our flag and our country.

Only in America ...

Only in America ... can a pizza get to your house faster than an ambulance.

Only in America ... are there handicap-parking places in front of a skating rink.

Only in America ... do people order double cheeseburgers, a large fry, and a diet cola.

Only in America ... do banks leave both doors open and then chain the pens to the counters.

Only in America ... do we leave cars worth thousands of dollars in the driveway and leave useless things and junk in boxes in the garage.

Only in America ... do we use answering machines to screen calls and then have call waiting so we won't miss a call from someone we didn't want to talk to in the first place.

Only in America ... do we buy hot dogs in packages of ten and buns in packages of eight.

Only in America ... are the least useful professions (professional athletes, movie actors, and entertainers) paid so disproportionately high compared to people with normal jobs.

Only in America ... do people buy domestic brand tires because they want to "buy American" and install them on their imported cars.

Only in America ... do the budgets for advertising nonessential items, like soft drinks, exceed the economies of many third-world nations.

Only in America ... do we use the word politics to describe the process so well. *Poli* in Latin meaning many and *tics* meaning bloodsucking creatures.

Life's Issues

Daily Praise

Dear God: Thank You for the love You've given me. Thank You for uniting with my spirit, and becoming one with me. I love You, Jesus. You're my all in all. You're my everything! You're the only thing I have to hang on to, to cling to—and I do. I cling to You desperately. Without You, without the breath of Your life, without the breath of Your Spirit, I know that I am absolutely nothing. Without You to hang on to, I'm nothing. There's nothing there without You. You're everything; I'm nothing. I'm nothing but a tool and a channel.

Words from Jesus

The greatness that God gives comes about from the tests, the trying times, and the trusting. The strength and the power that you seek does not come in the way that you would think. It does not come in the paths of glory as with man, but through the path of God—the lowly, humble path.

So in your time of suffering, look to Me. Call out to Me! Cling to My Words! Grasp them, hold on to them, for they are truth. For you to be the man or the woman of God that I would have you to be, you must have the understanding that My Word is truth and power and strength and might. It is My Word that saves you and strengthens you. It is My Word that encompasses you with protection. It is My Word that gives you the love that you seek. It is My Word that does all of these things. You must be connected to Me, and the root of that connection is My Word.

True Values

Nothing truly valuable arises from ambition or from a mere sense of duty; it stems rather from love and devotion towards men.
— *Albert Einstein*

Mahatma Gandhi identified the seven sins in the world as: wealth without work, pleasure before conscience, knowledge without character, commerce without morality, science without humanity, worship without sacrifice, and politics without principle.

We must understand spiritual truths and apply them to our modern life. We must draw strength from the almost forgotten virtues of simplicity, humility, contemplation, and prayer. It requires a dedication beyond science, beyond self, but the rewards are great and it is our only hope.— *Charles Lindbergh*

Measure wealth not by the things you have, but by the things you have that you wouldn't sell for money. — *Author Unknown*

An individual has not started living until he can rise above the narrow confines of his individualistic concerns to the broader concerns of all humanity. — *Martin Luther King, Jr.*

Life in time remains without meaning if it does not find its meaning in eternity. — *Nicolai Berdyaev*

The greatest use of life is to spend it for something that outlasts it.
— *William James*

Happiness is not so much in having as sharing. We make a living by what we get, but we make a life by what we give.
— *Norman MacEwan*

If life be short, then moderate your worldly cares and projects; do not cumber yourself with too much provision for a short voyage.
— *Author Unknown*

The person who tries to live alone will not succeed as a human being. His heart withers if it does not answer another heart. His mind shrinks away if he hears only the echoes of his own thoughts and finds no other inspiration. — *Pearl S. Buck*

The best and most beautiful things in the world cannot be seen or even touched. They must be felt within the heart.— *Helen Keller*

Life becomes harder for us when we live for others, but it also becomes richer and happier.— *Albert Schweitzer*

Ours is a world of nuclear giants and ethical infants. We know more about war than we know about peace, more about killing than we know about living. We have grasped the mystery of the atom and rejected the Sermon on the Mount.— *Omar N. Bradley*

That's God

Have you ever been just sitting there and all of a sudden, you feel like doing something nice for someone you care for? ... THAT'S GOD ... He talks to you through the Holy Spirit.

Have you ever been down and out and nobody seems to be around for you to talk to? ... THAT'S GOD ... He wants you to talk to Him.

Have you ever been thinking about somebody that you haven't seen in a long time and then next thing you know you see them or receive a phone call from them? ... THAT'S GOD ... there is no such thing as coincidence.

Have you ever received something wonderful that you didn't even ask for, like money in the mail, a debt that had mysteriously been cleared, or a coupon to a department store where you had just seen something you wanted, but couldn't afford? ... THAT'S GOD ... He knows the desire of your heart.

Have you even been in a situation and you had no clue how it was going to get better, but now you look back on it ... THAT'S GOD ... He passes us through tribulation to see a brighter day.

Don't tell GOD how big your storm is.
Tell the storm how big your GOD is!
NOW THAT'S GOD!!!!!!!!!!!!!!!

Important Recall Notice

Regardless of make or year, all units known as "human beings" are being recalled by the Manufacturer. This is due to a malfunction in the original prototype units code-named "Adam" and "Eve" resulting in the reproduction of the same defect in all subsequent units. This defect is technically termed, "Serious Internal Non-morality," but more commonly known as "SIN."

Some of the symptoms of the SIN defect:
(a) Loss of direction
(b) Lack of peace and joy
(c) Depression
(d) Foul vocal emissions
(e) Selfishness
(f) Ingratitude
(g) Fearfulness
(h) Rebellion
(i) Jealousy

The Manufacturer is providing factory-authorized repair service free of charge to correct the SIN defect. The Repair Technician, Christ, has most generously offered to bear the entire burden of the staggering cost of these repairs.

To repeat, there is no fee required. The number to call for repair in all areas is: P-R-A-Y-E-R.

Once connected, please upload the burden of SIN through the REPENTANCE procedure. Next, download ATONEMENT from the Repair Technician, Christ, into the heart component of the human unit.

No matter how big or small the SIN defect is, Christ will replace it with:
(a) Love
(b) Joy
(c) Peace
(d) Kindness
(e) Goodness
(f) Faithfulness
(g) Gentleness
(h) Patience
(i) Self-Control

Please see the operating manual, HOLY BIBLE, for further details on the use of these fixes.

As an added upgrade, the Manufacturer has made available to all repaired units a facility enabling direct monitoring and assistance from the resident Maintenance Technician, the Holy Ghost. Repaired units need only make Him welcome and He will take up residence on the premises.

WARNING: Continuing to operate a human being unit without corrections voids the Manufacturer's warranty, exposing the unit to dangers and problems too numerous to list, and will ultimately result in the human unit being incinerated.

Thank you for your attention. Please assist by notifying others of this important recall notice.

The Poetry Icon

6

The Lost Art of Reading Poetry

The Poetry Experience

Slow Down, Don't Dance So Fast

God Has a Plan

Smiling Is Infectious

Heaven's Grocery Store

Let Go and Let God

I Said a Prayer

The Lost Art of Reading Poetry

When is the last time you picked up a book of poetry and sat down to read it? Years ago, people treasured poetry. They taught it to their children, asking students to memorize entire poems in grammar school. These verses became dear to the children who learned them. They kept reciting these poems even into their elderly years. Poets were honored. Our grandparents valued the talents of a poet who could express deep feelings in the few verses of a poem.

Why have we abandoned the love for poetry? Perhaps you are still enamored with a poem. Are you one of those who can still read a poem and be moved to tears? This section includes some humor in verse form and some poignant thoughts expressed in rhyme and meter. Savor each poem like you would an expensive piece of chocolate. As you read the poem, let it filter through your mind slowly as you taste each word. Reread the lines that mean the most to you.

If you are drawn to a humorous poem, read it quickly, letting it do its work to relieve your stress and to touch your funny bone. Then read it aloud to a friend so that you can laugh together.

Now think of all your Internet friends with whom you would like to share each poem. Even people who don't think they like poetry will respond to the clear thinking and quick wit of the poetry found here.

The Poetry Experience

Slow Down, Don't Dance So Fast

Have you ever watched kids on a merry-go-round,
    or listened to the rain slapping on the ground?
Ever followed a butterfly's erratic flight,
    or gazed at the sun into the fading night?
You better slow down, don't dance so fast,
    time is short, the music won't last.
Do you run through each day on the fly?
    When you ask, "How are you?" do you hear the reply?
When the day is done, do you lie in your bed
    with the next hundred chores running through your head?
You'd better slow down, don't dance so fast,
    time is short, the music won't last.
Ever told your child, we'll do it tomorrow,
    and in your haste, not see his sorrow?
Ever lost touch, let a good friendship die,
    'cause you never had time to call and say "Hi"?
You'd better slow down, don't dance so fast,
    time is short, the music won't last.
When you run so fast to get somewhere,
    you miss half the fun of getting there.
When you worry and hurry through your day,
    it is like an unopened gift … thrown away.
Life is not a race, do take it slower.
    Hear the music, before the song is over.

God Has a Plan

When you're cast about by the storms of life,
When your days are filled with doubt and strife,
When nothing makes sense, when it's hard to stand,
Remember this—God has a plan.
God has a plan, keep clinging to this,
Forget your agenda and look to His.
He's kept every promise He ever made.
He's always on time, never early or late.
Time ticks by on a clock wound by Him,
And only He knows when time will end.
As you walk by faith, cling to His hand,
And remember this, God has a plan.

"We know that all things work together
for good to those who love God, to those
who are called according to His purpose."
(Romans 8:28)

Smiling Is Infectious

Smiling is infectious;
    you catch it like the flu.
When someone smiled at me today,
    I started smiling too.
I passed around the corner,
    and someone saw my grin.
When he smiled, I realized,
    I'd passed it on to him.
I thought about that smile,
    then I realized its worth.
A single smile, just like mine,
    could travel 'round the earth.

So if you feel a smile begin,
    don't leave it undetected.
Let's start an epidemic quick,
    and get the world infected!

Heaven's Grocery Store

As I was walking down life's highway many years ago, I came upon a sign that read, "Heavens Grocery Store."

When I got a little closer, the doors swung open wide. And when I came to myself, I was standing inside.

I saw a host of angels. They were standing everywhere. One handed me a basket and said, "My child, shop with care."

Everything a human needed was in that grocery store. And what you could not carry, you could come back for more.

First, I got some Patience. Love was in that same row. Further down was Understanding; you need that everywhere you go.

I got a box or two of Wisdom, and Faith—a bag or two. And Charity, of course; I would need some of that too.

I couldn't miss the Holy Ghost. He was all over the place. And then some Strength and Courage to help me run this race.

My basket was getting full, but I remembered I needed Grace. And then I chose Salvation for Salvation was for free. I tried to get enough of that to do for you and me.

Then I started to the counter to pay my grocery bill, because I thought I had everything to do the Master's will.

As I went up the aisle, I saw Prayer and put that in, because I knew when I stepped outside, I would run into sin.

Peace and Joy were plentiful, the last things on the shelf. Song and Praise were hanging near, so I just helped myself.

Then I said to the angel, "Now how much do I owe?" He smiled and said, "Just take them everywhere you go."

Again I asked, "Really now, how much do I owe?" "My child," he said, "Jesus paid your bill a long, long time ago."

Let Go and Let God

As children bring their broken toys,
with tears for us to mend,
I brought my broken dreams to God,
Because He is my friend.
But then instead of leaving Him
in peace to work alone,
I hung around and tried to help,
with ways that were my own.
At last, I snatched them back again,
And cried, "How can you be so slow?"
"My child," He said, "What could I do?
You never did let go."

I Said a Prayer

I said a prayer for you today
And know God must have heard.
I felt the answer in my heart
Although He spoke no word!
I didn't ask for wealth or fame,
I knew you wouldn't mind.
I asked Him to send treasures
Of a far more lasting kind.
I asked that He'd be near you
At the start of each new day.
To grant you health and blessings,
And friends to share your way.
I asked for happiness for you,
In all things great and small.
But it was for His loving care,
I prayed for most of all.

Password:
Special Days

7

Making Memories

Log on to the Holidays
The Reason for the Season
Gold Wrapping Paper

Remembering 9/11
The "Little" Things
Where Was God on 9/11?
Two Wolves
Unity

Other Special Days
Easter: The Heart of Easter
Easter: And They Crucified Him
*Thanksgiving: Martha Stewart Will Not Be
Dining With Us*

Making Memories

Melissa closed her scrapbook and put away her art supplies. She was finished with the entries she had added for the Christmas holiday. She sighed with a feeling of satisfaction. Then she booted up her computer and clicked onto her e-mail account. Immediately, she noticed a message from her daughter who lived halfway across the country. She opened the message and began reading the poem in the dialogue box. The poignant thoughts touched her heart. She knew exactly where she wanted to put this poem—in her scrapbook.

She printed off the poem and put some heart stickers along the margin of the paper. Then she reopened her scrapbook and took out the glue. She cut off the extra paper on the poem and glued it on the scrapbook page.

Then she looked in her "Favorite Places" file on her e-mail menu line. She shook her head, for she found nothing in there that would fit what she wanted to send to her daughter in return. If only she had a collection of things she could choose from.

Memories are made in many ways. Sometimes they come upon us unaware, like the time your granddaughter impulsively hugged you and said, "I love you." Other times, we find them where we expect them—in a Christmas dinner, on a cruise ship, at a wedding. Others we can make for ourselves—putting on a birthday party, taking a shut-in for a walk in a park, or reading a good book. Another way is to correspond through e-mails with wonderful stories and advice we forward to our friends.

This section of the book provides these kinds of memories for different holiday events. As each celebrated day approaches, find the messages that express what you want to say to your loved ones—and send them with your love.

Log on to the Holidays

The Reason for the Season

It's just a small white envelope, stuck among the branches of our Christmas tree. No name, no identification, no inscription. It has peeked through the branches of our tree for the past ten years or so.

It all began because my husband Mike hated Christmas, oh, not the true meaning of Christmas, but the commercial aspects of it. The overspending, the frantic running around at the last minute to get a tie for Uncle Harry, and the dusting powder for Grandma. The gifts given in desperation because you couldn't think of anything else.

Knowing he felt this way, I decided one year to bypass the usual shirts, sweaters, ties, and so forth. I reached for something special just for Mike. The inspiration came in an unusual way.

Our son Kevin, who was twelve then, was wrestling at the junior level at the school he attended. Shortly before Christmas, there was a non-league match against a team sponsored by an inner-city church, mostly black. These youngsters, dressed in sneakers so ragged that shoestrings seemed to be the only thing holding them together, presenting a sharp contrast to our boys in their spiffy blue-and-gold uniforms and sparkling new wrestling shoes.

As the match began, I was alarmed to see that the other team was wrestling without headgear (a kind of light helmet designed to protect a wrestler's ears). It was a luxury the ragtag team obviously could not afford. Well, we ended up walloping them by taking every weight class. And as each of their boys got up from the mat, he swaggered around in his tatters with false bravado, a kind of street pride that couldn't acknowledge defeat.

Mike, seated beside me, shook his head sadly, "I wish just one of them could have won," he said. "They have a lot of potential, but losing like this could take the heart right out of them."

Mike loved kids—all kids—and he knew them, having coached little league football, baseball, and lacrosse. That's when the idea for his present came. That afternoon, at a local sporting goods store I bought an assortment of wrestling headgear and shoes and sent them anonymously to the inner-city church. On Christmas Eve, I placed the envelope on the tree. The note inside told Mike what I had done and that this was his gift from me. His smile was the brightest thing about Christmas that year and in succeeding years.

For each Christmas, I followed the tradition—one year sending a group of mentally handicapped youngsters to a hockey game, another year a check to a pair of elderly brothers whose home had burned to the ground the week before Christmas, and on and on.

The envelope became the highlight of our Christmas. It was always the last thing opened on Christmas morning, and our children, ignoring their new toys, would stand with wide-eyed anticipation as their dad lifted the envelope from the tree to reveal its contents. As the children grew, the toys gave way to more practical presents, but the envelope never lost its allure, but the story doesn't end there.

You see, we lost Mike last year due to dreaded cancer. When Christmas rolled around, I was so wrapped in grief that I barely got the tree up. But Christmas Eve found me placing an envelope on the tree, and in the morning, it was joined by three more.

Each of our children, unbeknownst to the others, had placed an envelope on the tree for their dad. The tradition has grown and someday will expand even further with our grandchildren standing around the tree with wide-eyed anticipation, watching as the envelope is taken down.

Mike's spirit, like the Christmas spirit, will always be with us. May we all remember Christ, who is the reason for the season, and the true Christmas spirit this year and always.

Gold Wrapping Paper

Some time ago, a friend of mine punished his 3-year-old daughter for wasting a roll of gold wrapping paper. Money was tight, and he became infuriated when the child tried to decorate a box to put under the tree.

Nevertheless, the little girl brought the gift to her father the next morning and said, "This is for you, Daddy."

He was embarrassed by his earlier overreaction, but his anger flared again, when he found that the box was empty.

He yelled at her, "Don't you know that when you give someone a present, there's supposed to be something inside of it?"

The little girl looked up at him with tears in her eyes and said, "Oh, Daddy, it's not empty. I blew kisses into the box. All for you, Daddy."

The father was crushed. He put his arms around his little girl and begged her forgiveness. My friend told me that he kept that gold box by his bed for years. Whenever he was discouraged, he would take out an imaginary kiss and remember the love of the child who had put it there.

Remembering 9-11

The "Little" Things

One company invited the remaining members of other companies who had been decimated by the attack on the Twin Towers to share their available office space.

At a morning meeting, the head of security told stories of why these people were alive. And all the stories were just ... **the little things:**

As you might know, the head of the company survived that day *because his son started kindergarten.*

Another fellow was alive because *it was his turn to bring donuts.*

One woman was late because *her alarm clock didn't go off in time.*

One was late because of being stuck on the NJ Turnpike *because of an auto accident.*

One of them *missed his bus.*

One spilled food on her clothes and had to *take time to change.*

One's *car wouldn't start.*

One went back to *answer the telephone.*

One had *a child that dawdled* and didn't get ready as soon as he should have.

One *couldn't get a taxi.*

The one that struck me was the man who put on a new pair of shoes that morning, took the various means to get to work, but before he got there, he developed a blister on his foot. *He stopped at a drugstore to buy a Band-Aid.* That is why he is alive today!

Now when I am stuck in traffic, miss an elevator, turn back to answer a ringing telephone ... all the little things that annoy me. I think to myself, this is exactly where God wants me to be at this very moment.

Next time your morning seems to be going wrong, the children are slow getting dressed, you can't seem to find the car keys, or you hit every traffic light. Don't get mad or frustrated; God is at work watching over you.

May God continue to bless you with all those annoying little things and may you remember their possible purpose.

Where Was God on 9-11?

You say you will never forget where you were when you heard the news on September 11, 2001. Neither will I. I was on the 110th floor in a smoke-filled room with a man who called his wife to say "Good-bye." I held his fingers steady as he dialed. I gave him the peace to say, "Honey, I am not going to make it, but it is okay. I am ready to go."

I was with his wife when he called as she fed breakfast to their children. I held her up as she tried to understand his words and as she realized he wasn't coming home that night.

I was in the stairwell of the 23rd floor when a woman cried out to Me for help. "I have been knocking on the door of your heart for fifty years!" I said. "Of course, I will show you the way home— only believe in Me now."

I was at the base of the building with the priest ministering to the injured and devastated souls. I took him home to tend to his flock in heaven. He heard My voice and answered.

I was on all four of those planes, in every seat, with *every prayer*. I was with the crew as they were overtaken. I was in the very hearts of the believers there, comforting and assuring them that their faith has saved them.

I was in Texas, Kansas, London. I was standing next to you when you heard the terrible news. Did you sense Me?

I want you to know that I saw every face. I knew every name— though not all knew Me. Some met Me for the first time on the 86th floor. Some sought Me with their last breath.

Some couldn't hear Me calling to them through the smoke and flames: "Come to Me ... this way ... take My hand." Some chose to ignore Me for the final time.

But, I was there.

I did not place you in the Tower that day. You may not know why, but I do. However, if you had been there in that explosive moment in time, would you have reached for Me?

September 11, 2001, was not the end of the journey for you, but someday your journey will end. And I will be there for you as well. Seek Me now while I may be found. Then, at any moment, you know you are "ready to go."

I promise I will be in the stairwell of your final moments.

God

Two Wolves

A Native American grandfather was talking to his grandson about how he felt about the 9/11 tragedy. He said, "I feel as if I have two wolves fighting in my heart. One wolf is the vengeful, angry, violent one. The other wolf is the loving, compassionate one."

The grandson asked him, "Which wolf will win the fight in your heart?"

The grandfather answered, "The one I feed."

Unity

This e-mail is from an Ensign stationed aboard the USS Winston Churchill *to his father:*

Dear Dad,

Well, we are still with little direction as to what our next priority is. The remainder of our port visits, which were to be centered around maxliberty and goodwill to the United Kingdom, have all been cancelled. We have spent every day since the attacks going back and forth within imaginary boxes drawn in the ocean, standing high-security watches, and trying to make the best of our time. It hasn't been fun—that I must confess. And to be more honest, a lot of people are frustrated at the fact that either they can't be home or that we have no direction right now.

We have seen the articles and the photographs, and they are sickening. Being as isolated as we are, I don't think we comprehend the full scope of what is happening back home, but we are definitely feeling the effects.

About two hours ago, the junior officers were called to the bridge to conduct ship-handling drills. We were about to do "man overboard" when we got a call from the *Lutjens*, a German warship that was moored ahead of us on the pier in Plymouth England. (While in port there, the *Winston Churchill* and the *Lutjens* got together for a sports day/cookout on our fantail, and we made some pretty good friends.)

Now at sea the *Lutjens* called over to our bridge, requesting to pass us close on our port side to say good-bye. We prepared to render them honors on the bridgewing, and the Captain told the crew to come topside to wish them farewell. As they were making their approach, our Conning Officer announced through her binoculars that they were flying an American flag. As they came even closer, we saw that it was flying at half-mast. We all crowded our port side.

As the German ship came alongside, their entire crew was manning the rails in full dress blues, and they had made a huge sign that was displayed on the side—WE STAND BY YOU!

Dad, there was not a dry eye on our ship as we proudly cut our salutes. It was probably the most powerful thing I have seen in my entire life, and most of us fought to retain our composure.

You won't hear from me for awhile because we won't be at liberty to disclose our location over unsecured e-mail. But I must say that the German Navy did an incredible thing for this crew, and it has been the high point for us since the days of the attack. It's amazing that only a half century ago things were quite different. And to see the unity that is being demonstrated throughout Europe and the whole world makes us all feel proud to be out here doing our job.

Have a blessed day. Please pray for us as we are also praying for you. Contact me if I can be of help in anyway.

Other Special Days

Easter: The Heart of Easter

"Why do you seek the living among the dead? He is not here, but He has risen!" (Luke 24:5,6, NASB)

On the Sunday before Easter, *USA Weekend* magazine carried a full-page ad by Teleflora. It had a picture of a beautiful flower arrangement with a Peter Rabbit base. The headline of the ad read, "It wouldn't be Easter without him." The text read, "Celebrate the wonder and beauty of Spring with the Peter Rabbit™ Garden Bouquet." [*USA Weekend* magazine, inside cover, March 26-28, 1999]

Easter is coming. What is the center of that day for you? The world tries hard to draw attention to the nonessentials, but the heart of the day is the resurrection of Jesus Christ the Lord. Put Jesus in the center of your celebration. It wouldn't be Easter without Him!

Easter: "And They Crucified Him"

What is crucifixion? A medical doctor provides a physical description:

The cross is placed on the ground, and the exhausted man is quickly thrown backwards with his shoulders against the wood. The legionnaire feels for the depression at the front of the wrist. He drives a heavy, square wrought iron nail through the wrist deep into the wood. Quickly, he moves to the other side and repeats the action, being careful not to pull the arms too tightly, but to allow some flex and movement.

The cross is then lifted into place. The left foot is pressed backward against the right foot, and with both feet extended, toes down, a nail is driven through the arch of each foot, leaving the knees flexed. The victim is now crucified.

As he slowly sags down with more weight on the nails in the wrists, excruciating fiery pain shoots along the fingers and up the arms to explode in the brain. The nails in the wrists are putting pressure on the median nerves. As he pushes himself upward to avoid this stretching torment, he places the full weight of the nail through his feet. Again, he feels the searing agony of the nail tearing through the nerves between the bones of his feet. As the arms fatigue, cramps sweep through his muscles, knotting them deep, relentless, throbbing pain.

With these cramps comes the inability to push himself upward to breathe. Air can be drawn into the lungs but not exhaled. He fights to raise himself to get even one small breath. Finally, carbon dioxide builds up in the lungs and in the blood stream, and the cramps partially subside. Spasmodically, he is able to push himself upward to exhale and bring life-giving oxygen. He endures hours of limitless pain, cycles of twisting, joint-rending cramps, intermittent partial asphyxiation, searing pain as tissue is torn from his lacerated back as he moves up and down against rough timber.

Then another agony begins: a deep, crushing pain deep in the chest as the pericardium slowly fills with serums and begins to compress the heart. It is now almost over. The loss of tissue fluids has reached a critical level. The compressed heart is struggling to pump heavy, thick, sluggish blood into the tissues. The tortured lungs are making frantic efforts to gasp in small gulps of air. He can feel the chill of death creeping through his tissues.

Finally, he can allow his body to die.

All this the Bible records with the simple words, "and they crucified Him" (Mark 15:24). What wondrous love is this?

"He personally bore our sins in His [own] body on the tree [as on an altar and offered Himself on it], that we might die (cease to exist) to sin and live to righteousness, by His wounds you have been healed" (1 Peter 2:24).

Thanksgiving:
Martha Stewart Will Not Be Dining With Us

Martha Stewart will not be dining with us this Thanksgiving. I'm telling you in advance, so don't act surprised. Since Ms. Stewart won't be coming, I've made a few small changes:

Our sidewalk will not be lined with homemade, paper bag luminaries. After a trial run, it was decided that no matter how cleverly done, rows of flaming lunch sacks do not have the desired welcoming effect.

Once inside, our guests will note that the entry hall is not decorated with the swags of Indian corn and fall foliage I had planned to make. Instead, I've gotten the kids involved in decorating by having them track in colorful autumn leaves from the front yard. The mud was their idea.

The dining table will not be covered with expensive linens, fancy china, or crystal goblets. If possible, we will use dishes that match and everyone will get a fork. Since this IS Thanksgiving, we will refrain from using the plastic Peter Rabbit plate and the Santa napkins from last Christmas.

Our centerpiece will not be the tower of fresh fruit and flowers that I promised. Instead, we will be displaying a hedgehog-like decoration hand-crafted from the finest construction paper. The artist assures me it is a turkey.

We will be dining fashionably late. The children will entertain you while you wait. I'm sure they will be happy to share every choice comment I have made regarding Thanksgiving, Pilgrims, and the turkey hot-line. Please remember that most of these comments were made at 5:00 a.m. upon discovering that the turkey was still hard enough to cut diamonds.

As accompaniment to the children's recital, I will play a recording of tribal drumming. If the children should mention that I don't own a recording of tribal drumming, or that tribal drumming sounds suspiciously like a frozen turkey in a clothes dryer, ignore them. They are lying.

We toyed with the idea of ringing a dainty silver bell to announce the start of our feast, but in the end, we chose to keep our traditional method. We've also decided against a formal seating arrangement. When the smoke alarm sounds, please gather around the table and sit where you like. In the spirit of harmony, we will ask the children to sit at a separate table ... in a separate room ... next door.

Now, I know you have all seen pictures of one person carving a turkey in front of a crowd of appreciative onlookers. This will not be happening at our dinner. For safety reasons, the turkey will be carved in a private ceremony. I stress "private" meaning: Do not, under any circumstances, enter the kitchen to laugh at me. And do not send small, unsuspecting children to check on my progress. For you see, I have an electric knife—the turkey is unarmed. It stands to reason that I will eventually win. When I do, we will eat.

I would like to take this opportunity to remind my young diners that "passing the rolls" is not a football play. Nor is it a request to bean your sister in the head with warm tasty bread.

Oh, and one reminder for the adults: For the duration of the meal, and especially while in the presence of young diners, we will refer to the giblet gravy by its lesser-known name—cheese sauce. If a young diner questions you regarding the origins or type of cheese sauce, plead ignorance. Cheese sauce stains.

Before I forget, there is one last change. Instead of offering a choice between twelve different scrumptious desserts, we will be serving the traditional pumpkin pie, garnished with whipped cream and small fingerprints. You will still have a choice—take it or leave it.

Martha Stewart will not be dining with us this Thanksgiving. She probably won't come next year either. I am thankful.

Prayer: Message Board to Heaven

8

Where Do Your Prayers Go?

Prayer Stories
Answered Prayers
Opening Prayer
Be Prepared
Angel Assignment
Daddy's Empty Chair

Prayers for Today
A Prayer for Soldiers
Dear Lord
I Said a Prayer for You Today
Praying for One Another

Prayer Purposes
Prayer in School
Now I Sit Me Down in School
Stingy Faith
A.S.A.P.
One Question

Where Do Your Prayers Go?

A little girl once asked her mommy, "Where do my prayers go?"

Her mother hesitated before she answered. Then she said, "Some prayers go straight to heaven. Those are the ones that are said with a 'pure heart.' Some prayers just go to the ceiling. Those are the ones that are said with an 'impure heart.' Some prayers go to heaven and come back again. Those are the 'answered prayers.' Some prayers go to heaven and don't come back. Those are the times when God says, 'No.' And some prayers linger in front of heaven's throne before coming back. Those are the ones where God says, "Wait until I'm ready to answer."

The little girl sighed and said, "I think my prayer is still on the ceiling."

Her mother looked puzzled. "Why is that?"

"Because I prayed for a dog."

"Do you think God won't answer a prayer for a dog?"

"Yes, because I want the dog so that he will bite my brother!"

That little girl understood the purposes for prayer. We all sometimes pray with bad motives or for selfish reasons. But when our prayers are sincere, they tie into the power of God!

When we write down our prayers, we create a record of what we sent heavenward. But sometimes we just can't find the words to pray what we want. That's when having a prayer written by someone else helps. It can express exactly what we want to say. Or it can even express something deeper than we could imagine.

Use the prayers in this section with these goals in mind. Some of the entries will give us important information about praying. Other entries are prayers that we can use to uplift a friend or loved one.

When you send a prayer, make sure that you have also prayed the prayer for the person you have in mind. You will be amazed at the power of prayer when you do!

Prayer Stories

Answered Prayers

A missionary on furlough told this true story while visiting his home church in Michigan:

"While serving at a small field hospital in Africa, every two weeks I traveled by bicycle through the jungle to a nearby city for supplies. This was a journey of two days and required camping overnight at the halfway point.

"On one of these journeys, I arrived in the city where I planned to collect money from a bank, purchase medicine and supplies, and begin my two-day journey back to the field hospital. Upon arrival in the city, I observed two men fighting, one of whom had been seriously injured. I treated him for his injuries and at the same time talked to him about the Lord Jesus Christ.

"I then traveled two days, camping overnight, and arrived home without incident.

"Two weeks later, I repeated my journey. Upon arriving in the city, I was approached by the young man I had treated who told me that he had known I carried money and medicines. He said, 'Some friends and I followed you into the jungle, knowing you would camp overnight. We planned to kill you and take your money and drugs. But just as we were about to move into your camp, we saw that you were surrounded by 26 armed guards.'

"At this, I laughed and said, "I was certainly all alone out in that jungle campsite."

"The young man pressed the point, however, and said, 'No sir, I was not the only person to see the guards. My five friends also saw them, and we all counted them. It was because of those guards that we were afraid and left you alone.'"

At this point in the sermon, one of the men in the congregation jumped to his feet and interrupted the missionary, asking if he could tell him the exact day this happened. The missionary told the congregation the date, and the man who interrupted told him this story:

"On the night of your incident in Africa, it was morning here, and I was preparing to play golf. I was about to putt when I felt the urge to pray for you. In fact, the urging of the Lord was so strong that I called men in this church to meet with me here in the sanctuary to pray for you. Would all of those men who met with me on that day stand up?"

The men who had met together to pray that day stood up. The missionary wasn't concerned with who they were, he was too busy counting how many men he saw. There were 26.

This story is an incredible example of how the Spirit of the Lord moves in mysterious ways. If you ever feel such prodding, go along with it. Nothing is ever hurt by prayer except the gates of hell.

Opening Prayer

This interesting prayer was given in Kansas at the opening session of their Senate. It seems prayer still upsets some people.

When Minister Joe Wright was asked to open the new session of the Kansas Senate, everyone was expecting the usual generalities, but this is what they heard:

"Heavenly Father, we come before You today to ask Your forgiveness and to seek Your direction and guidance. We know Your Word says, 'Woe to those who call evil good,' but that is exactly what we have done. We have lost our spiritual equilibrium and reversed our values.

"We confess that: We have ridiculed the absolute truth of Your Word and called it Pluralism. We have exploited the poor and called it the Lottery. We have rewarded laziness and called it Welfare. We have killed our unborn and called it Choice. We have shot abortionists and called it Justifiable. We have neglected to discipline our children and called it building Self-esteem. We have abused power and called it Politics.

"We have coveted our neighbor's possessions and called it Ambition. We have polluted the air with profanity and pornography and called it Freedom of Speech. We have ridiculed the time-honored values of our forefathers and called it Enlightenment. Search us, Oh God, and know our hearts today; cleanse us from every sin and set us free.

"Guide and bless these men and women who have been sent to direct us to the center of Your will, and to openly ask these things in the name of Your Son, the living Savior, Jesus Christ. Amen."

The response was immediate. A number of legislators walked out during the prayer in protest.

In six short weeks, Central Christian Church, where Reverend Wright is pastor, logged more than 5,000 phone calls with only 47 of those calls responding negatively. The church is now receiving international requests for copies of this prayer from India, Africa, and Korea.

Commentator Paul Harvey aired this prayer on his radio program, *The Rest of the Story,* and received a larger response to this program than any other he has ever aired.

With the Lord's help, may this prayer sweep over our nation and wholeheartedly become our desire, so that we again can be called "one nation under God."

Be Prepared

This came from an airline employee concerned with getting the word out when the media fails to cover what really matters, such as whether we are ready to meet our maker.

Alaska Airlines Flight 261: An Alaska Airlines pilot involved in the investigation of the horrific crash of Alaska Flight 261 listened to the voice recorder from the downed plane. He reported that during the last nine minutes of the flight, the wife of the pastor from Monroe, Washington, could be heard sharing the gospel with the passengers over the plane's intercom system. Just before the final dive into the Pacific Ocean, she can be heard leading the Sinner's Prayer for Salvation.

The pilot also reported that the flight data recorded from the plane indicates that there is no good explanation for how the plane was able to stay in the air for those final nine minutes. But it did stay in the air until the pastor's wife had a chance to share the Gospel with the very attentive passengers and presumably lead many to salvation in Christ.

So in the midst of this tragedy, nearly 90 people had an extraordinary opportunity to get right with their maker just prior to meeting him.

Angel Assignment

Once upon a time, a child was waiting to be born. So, one day he asked God, "They tell me you are sending me to earth tomorrow, but being so small and helpless, how am I going to live there?"

God replied, "Among the many angels, I chose one for you. She will be waiting for you and will take care of you."

But the child wasn't sure he really wanted to go. "But tell me, here in Heaven, I don't do anything but sing and smile. That's enough for me to be happy."

God smiled. "Your angel will sing for you and will also smile for you every day. And you will feel your angel's love and be happy."

"And how am I going to be able to understand when people talk to me," the child continued, "if I don't know the language that men talk?"

God patted him on the head and said, "Your angel will tell you the most beautiful and sweet words you will ever hear, and with much patience and care, your angel will teach you how to speak." The child was sad. "And what am I going to do when I want to talk to you?"

But God had an answer for that question too. "Your angel will place your hands together and will teach you how to pray."

The baby then turned to God and asked, "I've heard that on earth there are bad men. Who will protect me?"

"Your angel will defend you even if it means risking her life!"

"But I will always be sad, because I will not see you anymore," the child continued warily.

God smiled on the young one. "Your angel will always talk to you about me and will teach you the way for you to come back to me, even though I will always be next to you."

At that moment, peace flooded Heaven, but voices from earth could already be heard. The child knew he had to start on his journey very soon. He asked God one more question, "Oh, God, if I am about to leave now, please tell me my angel's name."

God touched the child on the shoulder just before he departed and answered, "Your angel's name is of no importance. You will simply call her 'Mom'."

Daddy's Empty Chair

A man's daughter had asked the local minister to come and pray with her father. When the minister arrived, he found the man lying in bed with his head propped up on two pillows. An empty chair sat beside his bed. The minister assumed that the old fellow had been informed of his visit.

"I guess you were expecting me," he said.

"No, who are you?" said the father.

The minister told him his name and then remarked, "I saw the empty chair and I figured you knew I was going to show up."

"Oh yeah, the chair," said the bedridden man. "Would you mind closing the door?"

Puzzled, the minister shut the door. "I have never told anyone this, not even my daughter," said the man, "but all of my life I have never known how to pray. At church, I used to hear the pastor talk about prayer, but it went right over my head."

"I abandoned any attempt at prayer," the old man continued, "until one day four years ago, my best friend said to me, 'Johnny, prayer is a simple matter of having a conversation with Jesus. Here's what I suggest. Sit down in a chair, place an empty chair in front of you, and in faith see Jesus on the chair. It's not spooky because he promised to be with you always. Then just speak to him in the same way you're doing with me right now.'

"So, I tried it, and I've liked it so much that I do it a couple of hours every day. I'm careful though. If my daughter saw me talking to an empty chair, she'd either have a nervous breakdown or send me off to the funny farm."

The minister was deeply moved by the story and encouraged the old man to continue on the journey. Then he prayed with him, anointed him with oil, and returned to the church.

Two nights later, the daughter called to tell the minister that her daddy had died that afternoon.

"Did he die in peace?" he asked.

"Yes, when I left the house about two o'clock he called me over to his bedside, told me he loved me, and kissed me on the cheek. When I got back from the store an hour later, I found him dead. But there was something strange about his death. Apparently, just before Daddy died, he leaned over and rested his head on the chair beside the bed. What do you make of that?"

The minister wiped a tear from his eye and said, "I wish we could all go like that."

Prayer is one of the best free gifts we receive.

I asked God for water, He gave me an ocean. I asked God for a flower, He gave me a garden. I asked God for a friend, He gave me all of YOU.

Prayers for Today

A Prayer for Soldiers

"Lord, hold our troops in your loving hands. Protect them as they protect us. Bless them and their families for the selfless acts they perform for us in our time of need. I ask this in the name of Jesus, our Lord, and Savior. Amen."

Please stop for a moment and say a prayer for our troops in Afghanistan and Iraq. Of all the gifts you could give a U.S. soldier, prayer is the very best one.

Dear Lord

Dear Lord,

So far today, I am doing all right. I have not gossiped, lost my temper, or been greedy, grumpy, nasty, selfish, or self-indulgent. I have not whined, complained, cursed, eaten any chocolate, or charged anything on my credit cards. However, I am going to get out of bed soon, and I will need a lot more help after that.

Amen.

I Said a Prayer for You Today

I said a prayer for you today
    and know God must have heard.
I felt the answer in my heart
    although He spoke no word.
I didn't ask for wealth or fame,
    I knew you wouldn't mind.
I asked Him to send treasures
    of a far more lasting kind!
I asked that He'd be near you
    at the start of each new day
to grant you health and blessing
    and friends to share your way!
I asked for happiness for you
    in all things great and small.
But it was for His loving care
    I prayed for most of all!
Amen.

Praying for One Another

Father, I ask you to bless my friends reading this right now. I am asking You to minister to their spirits at this very moment. Where there is pain, give them Your peace and mercy. Where there is self-doubting, release a renewed confidence in Your ability to work through them. Where there is tiredness or exhaustion, I ask You to give them understanding, patience, and strength as they learn submission to your leading. Where there is spiritual stagnation, I ask You to renew them by revealing Your nearness, and by drawing them into greater intimacy with You.

Where there is fear, reveal Your love and release to them Your courage. Where there is sin blocking them, reveal it, and break its hold over my friends' lives. Bless their finances, give them greater vision, and raise up leaders and friends to support and encourage them. Give them discernment to recognize the evil forces, and reveal to them the power they have in You to defeat these forces.

I ask You to do these things for my friends and I ask You to bless and protect America, in Jesus' name. Amen.

Prayer Purposes

Prayer in School

The Prayer ...

Dear God,
Why didn't you save the school children in Littleton, Colorado?
Sincerely, Concerned Student

The Reply ...

Dear Concerned Student:
I am not allowed in schools.
Sincerely, God

Now I Sit Me Down in School

This was written by a teen in Bagdad, Arizona.

Now I sit me down in school
Where praying is against the rule

For this great nation under God
Finds mention of Him very odd.

If Scripture now the class recites,
It violates the Bill of Rights.
Anytime my head I bow
Becomes a federal matter now.

Our hair can be purple, orange or green,
That's no offense; it's a freedom scene.
The law is specific; the law is precise.
Prayers spoken aloud are a serious vice.

For praying in a public hall
Might offend someone with no faith at all.
In silence alone we must mediate.
God's name is prohibited by the state.

We're allowed to cuss and dress like freaks
And pierce our noses, tongues, and cheeks.
They've outlawed guns, but first the Bible.
To quote the Good Book makes me liable.

We can elect a pregnant Senior Queen,
And the "unwed daddy" our Senior King.
It's "inappropriate" to teach right from wrong,
We're taught that such "judgments" do not belong.

We can get our condoms and birth controls,
Study witchcraft, vampires, and totem poles.
But the Ten Commandments are not allowed;
No word of God must reach this crowd.

It's scary here I must confess.
When chaos reigns, the school's a mess.

So, Lord, this silent plea I make:
Should I be shot; my soul please take!
Amen

"I can do all things through Christ that strengthens me"
(Philippians 4:13).

Stingy Faith

A group of men went out on a boat to do some fishing in the ocean. A tremendous storm brewed and threatened to sink the boat. All the men began praying to God to save them, except one. This man was irreligious, and it had been years since he had entered a church. Upon the group's insistence, the ungodly man sent up the following prayer: "O Lord, I have not asked you for anything in fifteen years. If you will get us out of this storm and safely to land, I promise not to bother you for another fifteen years."

Do you have stingy faith? Do you only pray to the Lord when you absolutely have to? God is not bothered by your requests. In fact, He delights when you bring everything to Him in prayer. He truly cares, and don't worry about being a burden to God—you're no bother!

"Cast all your anxiety on Him because He cares for you" (1 Peter 5:7, NIV).

A.S.A.P.

Ever wonder about the abbreviation A.S.A.P? Generally, we think of it in terms of even more hurry and stress in our lives. Maybe if we think of this abbreviation in a different manner, we will begin to find a new way to deal with those rough days along the way.

There's work to do, deadlines to meet.
You've got no time to spare,
But as you hurry and scurry,
ASAP–Always Say a Prayer.

In the midst of family chaos,
Quality time is rare.
Do your best; let God do the rest,
ASAP–Always Say a Prayer.

It may seem like your worries
Are more than you can bear.
Slow down and take a breather,
ASAP–Always Say a Prayer.

God knows how stressful life is;
He wants to ease our cares,
And He'll respond to all your needs,
ASAP–Always Say a Prayer.

One Question

NOW that the President has called us to prayer …
NOW that Congress has called us to prayer …
NOW that our Governor has called us to prayer …
NOW that the city Mayor has called us to prayer …
NOW that the "liberal" media and most other branches of our American society have called us to prayer …
AND NOW that our churches are assembling in special prayer …
"Honorable" Justices of the Supreme Court, I have only one question …
Would it be O.K. to pray in our schools … ?

An American Citizen and Christian

FAQs for the Inspirational Side of Life

9

What Do You Want to Know?

Advice from God
Memo from God
Interview with God

Wisdom for Living
Your Gift to God
When Your Burden Is Overwhelming
An Everyday Survival Kit
Looking At It Differently

Keeping It in Perspective
Subject: The Professor and the Student
The Gifts
The Global Village
The Most Useless Day
Lessons from Noah's Life
My Commitment as a Christian

Words to Remember

The Center of the Bible

Books of the Bible–Their Meaning

A Positive Thought

Rules for Happy Living

Stories to Live By

The Card Room

The Old Mule

The Deck of Cards

Tips for a Fuller Life

Eating & Drinking

Thought You Might Like This

Three Things

What Do You Want to Know?

What are your "Frequently Asked Questions" (FAQs)? What do you want to ask your supervisor at work? What would you like to ask your children or your parents? What would you like to ask the computer tech person you contact on the telephone?

"Frequently Asked Questions" are now a familiar part of most websites. But these kinds of questions pale when compared to the questions most frequently asked about life. For example: Why don't we receive immediate answers to our prayers? Why should I consider myself blessed? How can I serve Jesus at work? How can I survive my everyday life?

The entries in this section cover these and so many more fascinating topics. Some of the entries treat serious subjects with a dash of humor. Others tell heart-wrenching stories that illustrate an important point. A poem may touch your heart or an adage may help you solve a problem. The questions you find answers to will give vital information to the subject at hand, a pathway to solve problems, or a way to soothe a hurting heart.

Advice from God

Memo from God

To: YOU
Date: TODAY
From: THE BOSS
Subject: YOURSELF
Reference: LIFE

I am God.

Today I will be handling all of your problems. Please remember that I do not need your help.

If life happens to deliver a situation to you that you cannot handle, do not attempt to resolve it. Kindly put it in the SFGTD (something for God to do) box. It will be addressed in My time, not yours. Once the matter is placed into the box, do not hold on to it.

If you find yourself struck in traffic, don't despair. Many people in this world consider driving an unheard-of privilege.

Should you have a bad day at work, think of the man who has been out of work for years. Should you despair over a relationship gone bad, think of the person who has never known what it's like to love and be loved in return.

Should you grieve the passing of another weekend, think of the woman in dire straits, working twelve hours a day, seven days a week to feed her children.

Should your car break down, leaving you miles away from assistance, think of the paraplegic who would love the opportunity to take that walk.

Should you notice a new gray hair in the mirror, think of the cancer patient in chemo who wishes he/she had hair to examine.

Should you find yourself at a loss and pondering what is life all about, ask, "What is my purpose?" Be thankful. Many don't live long enough to get the opportunity.

Should you find yourself the victim of other people's bitterness, ignorance, smallness, or insecurities, remember that things could be worse. You could be them!!!!

Should you decide to send this to a friend, you might brighten someone's day!

Interview with God

"Come in," God said. "So, you would like to interview Me?"

"If you have the time," I said.

God smiled and said, "My time is eternity and is enough to do everything. What questions do you have in mind to ask me?"

"What surprises you most about mankind?"

God answered, "That they get bored of being children, are in a rush to grow up, and then long to be children again.

"That they lose their health to make money, and then lose their money to restore their health.

"That by thinking anxiously about the future, they forget the present. So that they live neither for the present nor the future.

"That they live as if they will never die, and they die as if they had never lived ..."

God's hands took mine, and we were silent for a while, and then I asked, "As a parent, what are some of life's lessons You want Your children to learn?"

God replied with a smile, "To learn that they cannot make anyone love them. What they can do is to let themselves be loved.

"To learn that what is most valuable is not what they have in their lives, but who they have in their lives.

"To learn that it is not good to compare themselves to others. All will be judged individually on their own merits, not as a group on a comparison basis!

"To learn that a rich person is not the one who has the most, but is one who needs the least.

"To learn that it only takes a few seconds to open profound wounds in persons we love, and that it takes many years to heal them.

"To learn to forgive by practicing forgiveness.

"To learn that there are people who love dearly, but simply do not know how to express or show their feelings.

"To learn that money can buy everything but happiness.

"To learn that two people can look at the same thing and see it differently.

"To learn that a true friend is someone who knows everything about him—and likes him anyway.

"To learn that it is not always enough that they be forgiven by others, but that they have to forgive themselves."

I sat there for a while enjoying the moment. I thanked Him for His time and for all that He has done for my family and me.

He replied, "Anytime. I'm here 24 hours a day. All you have to do is ask for me, and I'll answer."

People will forget what you said. People will forget what you did, but people will never forget how you made them feel.

Wisdom for Living

Your Gift to God

The only things you own are your body and soul. The only thing you have is yourself. The only thing you are granted is time. Make the best of it. Remember: You are God's gift to yourself. What you make of yourself is your gift to God.

When Your Burden is Overwhelming

"Cast your burden on the Lord ... " (Psalm 55:22).

We must recognize the difference between burdens that are right for us to bear and burdens that are wrong. We should never bear the burdens of sin and doubt, but there are some burdens placed on us by God, which He does not intend to lift off. God wants us to roll them back on Him—to literally "cast your burden," which He has given you, "on the Lord ..." If we set out to serve God and do His work, but get out of touch with Him, the sense of responsibility we feel will be overwhelming and defeating. But if we will only roll back on God the burdens He has placed on us, He will take away that immense feeling of responsibility, replacing it with an awareness and understanding of Himself and His presence.

Many servants set out to serve God with great courage and with the right motives. But with no intimate fellowship with Jesus Christ, they are soon defeated. They do not know what to do with their burden, and it produces weariness in their lives. Others will see this and say, "What a sad end to something that had such a great beginning!"

"Cast your burden on the Lord." You have been bearing it all, but you need to deliberately place one end on God's shoulder. "... the government will be upon His shoulder" (Isaiah 9:6). Commit to God whatever burden He has placed on you. Don't just cast it aside, but put it over onto Him, placing yourself there too. You will see that your burden is then lightened by the sense of companionship. But you should never try to separate yourself from your burden.

(Oswald Chambers, *My Utmost for His Highest*)

An Everyday Survival Kit

Toothpick
Rubber Band
Pencil
Eraser
Chewing Gum
Mint
Candy Kiss
Tea Bag

Here's why:

Toothpick—to remind you to pick out the good qualities in others (Matthew 7:1).

Rubber Band—to remind you to be flexible, things might not always go the way you want, but they will work out (Romans 8:28).

Band Aid—to remind you to heal hurt feelings, yours or someone else's (Colossians 3:12-14).

Pencil—to remind you to list your blessings every day (Ephesians 1:3).

Eraser—to remind you that everyone makes mistakes, and it's okay (Genesis 50:15-21).

Chewing Gum—to remind you to stick with it and you can accomplish anything (Philippians 4:13).

Mint—to remind you that you are worth a mint to your heavenly Father (John 3:16,17).

Candy Kiss—to remind you that everyone needs a kiss or a hug every day (1 John 4:7).

Tea Bag—to remind you to relax daily and go over that list of God's blessings (1 Thessalonians 5:18).

To the world, you may just be somebody, but to somebody, you may just be the world!

Looking At It Differently

This is an eye opener; some probably never thought or looked at this Psalm in this way, even though they say it over and over again.

The Lord is my Shepherd.
That's Relationship!
I shall not want.
That's Supply!
He maketh me to lie down in green pastures.
That's Rest!
He leadeth me beside the still waters.
That's Refreshment!
He restoreth my soul.
That's Healing!
He leadeth me in the paths of righteousness.
That's Guidance!
For His name sake.
That's Purpose!

Yea, though I walk through the valley of the shadow of death.
That's Testing!
I will fear no evil.
That's Protection!
For Thou art with me.
That's Faithfulness!
Thy rod and Thy staff they comfort me.
That's Discipline!
Thou preparest a table before me in the presence of mine enemies.
That's Hope!
Thou anointest my head with oil.
That's Consecration!
My cup runneth over.

That's Abundance!
Surely goodness and mercy shall follow me all the days of my life.
That's Blessing!
And I will dwell in the house of the Lord.
That's Security!
Forever …
That's Eternity!

Keeping It in Perspective

Subject: The Professor and the Student

The university professor challenged his students with this question: "Did God create everything that exists?"

A student bravely replied "Yes, he did!"

"God created everything?" The professor asked.

"Yes sir," the student replied.

The professor answered, "If God created everything, then God created evil since evil exists, and according to the principle that our works define who we are, then God is evil."

The student became quiet before such an answer.

The professor was quite pleased with himself and boasted to the students that he had proven once more that Christian faith was a myth.

Another student raised his hand and said, "Can I ask you a question professor?"

"Of course," replied the professor.

The student stood up and asked, "Professor, does cold exist?"

"What kind of a question is this? Of course, it exists. Have you never been cold?"

The students snickered at the young man's question.

The young man replied, "In fact sir, cold does not exist. According to the laws of physics, what we consider cold is in reality the absence of heat. Every body or object is susceptible to study when it has or transmits energy, and heat is what makes a body or matter have or transmit energy. Absolute zero (-460 degrees F) is the total absence of heat; all matter becomes inert and incapable of reaction at that temperature. Cold does not exist. We have created this word to describe how we feel if we have no heat."

The student continued. "Professor, does darkness exist?"

The professor responded, "Of course it does."

The student replied, "Once again you are wrong sir, darkness does not exist either. Darkness is in reality the absence of light. Light we can study, but not darkness. In fact, we can use Newton's prism to break white light into many colors and study the various wavelengths of each color. You cannot measure darkness. A simple ray of light can break into a world of darkness and illuminate it. How can you know how dark a certain space is? You measure the amount of light present. Isn't this correct? Darkness is a term used by man to describe what happens when there is no light present."

Finally, the young man asked the professor, "Sir, does evil exist?"

Now uncertain, the professor responded, "Of course, as I have already said. We see it every day. It is in the daily example of man's inhumanity to man. It is in the multitude of crime and violence everywhere in the world. These manifestations are nothing else but evil."

To this the student replied, "Evil does not exist sir, or at least it does not exist unto itself. Evil is simply the absence of God. It is just like darkness and cold, a word that man has created to describe the absence of God. God did not create evil. Evil is not like faith, or love that exist just as does light and heat. Evil is the result of what happens when man does not have God's love present in his heart. It's like the cold that comes when there is no heat or the darkness that comes when there is no light."

The professor sat down.

The young man is thought to have been Albert Einstein!

The Gifts

The Gift of Listening
But you must *really* listen. No interrupting, no daydreaming, no planning your response. Just listening.

The Gift of Affection
Be generous with appropriate hugs, kisses, pats on the back, and handholds. Let these small actions demonstrate the love you have for family and friends.

The Gift of Laughter
Clip cartoons. Share articles and funny stories. Your gift will say, "I love to laugh with you."

The Gift of a Written Note
It can be a simple "Thanks for the help" note or a full sonnet. A brief, handwritten note may be remembered for a lifetime, and may even change a life.

The Gift of a Compliment
A simple and sincere "You look great in red," "You did a super job," or "That was a wonderful meal" can make someone's day.

The Gift of a Favor
Every day, go out of your way to do something kind.

The Gift of Solitude
There are times when we want nothing better than to be left alone. Be sensitive to those times and give the gift of solitude to others.

The Gift of a Cheerful Disposition
The easiest way to feel good is to extend a kind word to someone.

The Global Village

If we could shrink the earth's population to a village of precisely 100 people, with all the existing human ratios remaining the same, it would look something like the following. There would be:

57 Asians

21 Europeans

14 from the Western Hemisphere (North and South America)

8 Africans

52 would be female

48 would be male

70 would be nonwhite

30 would be white

70 would be non-Christian

30 would be Christian

6 people would possess 59 percent of the entire world's wealth and all six would be from the United States

80 would live in substandard housing

70 would be unable to read

50 would suffer from malnutrition

1 would be near death

1 would be near birth

1 (yes, only 1) would have a college education

1 would own a computer

When one considers our world from such a compressed perspective, the need for acceptance, understanding, and education becomes glaringly apparent.

The Most Useless Day

The most useless day of all is that in which we have not laughed. We are told that laughter is sunshine filling a room.

And where there is laughter, there also is life.

They say that people who laugh a lot, live longer than do the sour-faced.

When we laugh together, gratitude comes more easily, companionship thrives, and all praise is sincere.

Laughter brings us joy that cannot be bought.

Such joy is with us throughout each day.

To hoard joy, to hide it away deep within us, away from others, will make us lonely misers.

We cannot buy or trade for joy, but we can give or receive it as a gift.

Laughter's joy celebrates the moment we are living right now.

It is a gift we must share, or it will wither and die.

Shared, it grows and thrives, and always returns to us when we need it most.

Lessons from Noah's Life

1. He was a man who stood for righteousness in an unrighteous generation.

Noah lived in a time when there was incredible darkness in the world, yet Noah chose to walk in the light. At times, he must have felt terribly alone. Yet, he was never forsaken. His life was blessed by God's grace. The very same grace that God extended to Noah, He extends to us. Can we do any less than to live for Him?

2. He was given an impossible task.

He was to collect two of every kind of animal on the planet and put them in the ark! This was an immense project. How could he possibly do it? At times, the task of being salt and light can seem overwhelming. Yet we serve the God who is the great I AM, who gently whispers in our ear, "Nothing is impossible with me."

3. He had to let go and let God. Noah could not do the impossible task of collecting all those animals, but God could. Noah just let go and let God bring the animals to him. We can let go and let God! Is anything too hard for Him? Yes, sin's darkness is alive and well, but so is Jesus Christ. We are the light of the world. God sent a great Light in the form of an infant child. May you and I be faithful to walk in that Light as we seek to follow the Son!

"Let us not grow weary in doing good, for at the proper time we will reap a harvest if we do not give up" (Galatians 6:9).

(Christianity Online's Women to Women Newsletter, December 1998)

My Commitment as a Christian

I'm part of the fellowship of the unashamed. I have stepped over the line. The decision has been made. I'm a disciple of Jesus Christ. I won't look back, let up, slow down, back away, or be still. My past is redeemed, my present makes sense, and my future is secure. I'm finished and done with low living, sight walking, small planning, smooth knees, colorless dreams, tamed visions, mundane talking, cheap living, and dwarfed goals.

I no longer need preeminence, prosperity, position, promotions, plaudits, or popularity. I don't have to be right, first, tops, recognized, praised, regarded, or rewarded. I now live by faith, lean on His presence, walk by patience, live by prayer, and labor by power.

My face is set, my gait is fast, my goal is heaven, my road is reliable, my mission is clear. I cannot be bought, deluded, or delayed. I will not flinch in the face of sacrifice, hesitate in the presence of the adversary, negotiate at the table of the enemy, or meander in the maze of mediocrity.

I won't give up, shut up, let up, until I have stayed up, stored up, prayed up, paid up, preached up for the cause of Christ. I am a disciple of Jesus. I must go till He comes, give till I drop, preach till all know, and work till He stops me. And when He comes for His own, He will have no problem recognizing me ... my banner will be clear.

These lines were penned by a young pastor in Africa and tacked to a wall in his house.

Words to Remember

The Center of the Bible

What is the shortest chapter in the Bible? Answer: Psalms 117
What is the longest chapter in the Bible? Answer: Psalms 119
What chapter is in the center of the Bible? Answer: Psalms 118
Fact: There are 594 chapters before Psalms 118.
Fact: There are 594 chapters after Psalms 118.
Add these numbers up and you get 1188.
What is the center verse in the Bible? Answer: Psalms 118:8
Does this verse say something significant about God's perfect will for our lives?
The next time someone says they would like to find God's perfect will for their lives and that they want to be in the center of His will, just send them to the center of His Word!
Psalms 118:8 (NKJV) "It is better to trust in the LORD than to put confidence in man."
Isn't that odd how this all worked out or was God in the center of it?

Books of the Bible—Their Meaning

Old Testament

GENESIS is Greek for the Hebrew title, which means, "In the Beginning."

EXODUS, or "Going Out," records the departure of Israel from Egypt.

LEVITICUS refers to the work and ministry of the Levites, the priestly tribe.

NUMBERS describes the taking of the Hebrew census.

DEUTERONOMY means "The Repetition of the Law."

JOSHUA. The Book of Joshua was named for Joshua—soldier, statesman, and successor of Moses.

JUDGES was the title given to the leaders of Israel after Joshua to the time of Saul.

RUTH. The Book of Ruth is the most beautiful story of the Old Testament, introducing the ancestry of David.

I AND II SAMUEL. The two books of Samuel are one in the Hebrew and contain the history of Israel from Samuel to David.

I AND II KINGS. The two books of Kings, originally one book, contain the history of Israel from the reign of Solomon to the Exile.

I AND II CHRONICLES. The two books of Chronicles, originally one book, contain genealogies and the history of Israel from the time of the Kings to the return from the Exile.

EZRA AND NEHEMIAH, originally one book, contain the history of Israel from the return from Babylon to the restoration of the Temple.

ESTHER. The Book of Esther tells of the Jews under Persian rule and the origin of the feast of Purim.

JOB. The Book of Job is the world's greatest dramatic presentation of the problem of suffering.

PSALMS. Psalms is the hymn book of the Hebrew people, arranged in five books, or divisions.

PROVERBS. The Proverbs is one of the "wisdom" books of the Old Testament.

ECCLESIASTES is from the Greek word translating the Hebrew Koheleth, commonly called "The Preacher," and is the second of the "wisdom" books.

SONG OF SOLOMON. This book is also called "The Song of Songs," and is about romantic love.

LAMENTATIONS. The Lamentations of Jeremiah was a dirge sung over the destruction of Jerusalem.

ISAIAH. Isaiah was the greatest preacher among the prophets.

EZEKIEL. Ezekiel was the prophet of the Exile. He proclaimed the doctrine of individual responsibility.

DANIEL. The Book of Daniel is classed with The Revelation of John as an apocalypse, or revelation of the future.

HOSEA. Hosea was the prophet of love.

JOEL. Joel was the prophet of judgment.

AMOS. Amos was the prophet of justice.

OBADIAH. Obadiah was the prophet of the reconstruction.

JONAH. Jonah was the prophet of universal salvation.

MICAH. Micah was the prophet of moral righteousness.

NAHUM. Nahum was the prophet of a higher nationalism.

HABAKKUK. Habakkuk was the prophet of the triumphs of faith.

ZEPHANIAH. Zephaniah was the prophet of reform.

HAGGAI. Haggai was the prophet of the second Temple.

ZECHARIAH. Zechariah was the prophet of the Restoration.

MALACHI. Malachi was the prophet of the coming Christ.

New Testament

MATTHEW. Matthew writes about the Kingship of Christ.

MARK. Mark writes about Jesus as the Servant of God and man.

LUKE. This book emphasizes the universal grace of God and Jesus as the "Son of Man."

JOHN. This book inspires faith in Jesus Christ as the Son of God.

ACTS. Luke writes about the history and development of the early Church.

ROMANS. Written by Paul to the church at Rome, the first eleven chapters are doctrinal; the last five, practical.

I CORINTHIANS. Paul writes to the church in Corinth to meet certain difficult religious and moral problems.

II CORINTHIANS. This book reflects the favorable reception of Paul's first letter and discusses other religious and moral issues.

GALATIANS. This is Paul's most passionate letter, in which he champions the gospel of grace.

EPHESIANS. This is a circular letter written to the churches in Ephesus and in Asia.

PHILIPPIANS. This is the most personal of all Paul's letters.

COLOSSIANS. This book was written to refute heresies. It is the most philosophical of Paul's epistles.

I THESSALONIANS. This is the earliest of Paul's letters, dealing particularly with the Second Advent.

II THESSALONIANS. Paul exhorts Christians to fidelity in preparation for the coming of Christ.

I TIMOTHY. This book is the first of the so-called "Pastoral Epistles"–Paul's advice to Timothy, his son in the faith.

II TIMOTHY. This is the second of the "Pastoral Epistles," written shortly before Paul's martyrdom.

TITUS. This is the third of the "Pastoral Epistles" written by Paul to his friend Titus.

PHILEMON. This book is the most gentlemanly letter ever written by the most perfect gentleman.

HEBREWS. Often ascribed to Paul, Hebrews is anonymous. Its theme is "Christianity in Christ."

JAMES. James, the brother of our Lord, presents the gospel as the royal law of Christ.

I PETER. This book was written by Peter the apostle to encourage the Church passing through severe persecution.

II PETER. Peter defends the true Christian faith against current false teaching.

I JOHN. This book was written by John the apostle, to Christian friends, whom he calls his children.

II JOHN. This book contains warnings against false teachers.

III JOHN. John wrote this book to Gaius, commending him for his Christian faith and love.

JUDE. Jude, the brother of our Lord, warns the Church against immoral practices.

REVELATION. The Revelation of John is classed with The Book of Daniel as an apocalypse. It presents Christianity as the one triumphant religion.

A Positive Thought

If God had a refrigerator, your picture would be on it.

If He had a wallet, your photo would be in it.

He sends you flowers every spring, and a sunrise every morning.

Whenever you want to talk, He'll listen.

He could live anywhere in the universe, and He chose your heart.

What about the Christmas gift He sent you in Bethlehem; not to mention that Friday at Calvary?

Face it, He really loves you a lot.

I thought this was mighty special, just like you.

Rules for Happy Living

1. Count your blessing, not your troubles. Other people don't need your troubles; they have enough of their own (Malachi 3:10).

2. Live one day at a time. You can control and conquer any sin if you will learn to live one day at a time (James 4:13-15).
3. Learn to say, "I love you." Break the alabaster box of kindness over as many people as you can (Mark 14:3-6).
4. Learn to be a giver and not a getter. If you're failing to get out of life what you want, it is because you are expecting to get instead of give (Luke 6:38).
5. See good in everyone and everything. Be a "good" seeker, and not a fault finder (Matthew 7:1-5).
6. Pray every day. Reserve a time in your day to thank God for His blessing and ask for His guidance (Luke 18:1).
7. Do at least one good deed each day. Plant the seed of goodness, and it will produce after its own kind (Acts 10:38).
8. Learn to prioritize. All things have a place in life. Keep important things in first place (Matthew 6:33).
9. Let nothing bother you. We let too many little things destroy our peace of mind. We even allow imaginary things to bother us (Philippians 4:7).
10. Practice the "do it now" habit. The road to hell is paved with good intentions (2 Corinthians 6:1,2).
11. Fill your life with good. Clean out the trash, and fill your life with good thoughts and deeds (Philippians 4:8).
12. Learn to laugh and to cry. More than 70 percent of all physical ills could be overcome if we could learn this (Romans 12:15).
13. Learn to practice the happiness habit. Learn to smile, and the world will smile with you (Philippians 4:4).
14. Learn to fear nothing and no one. Think of your own powers, and not weaknesses. Crowd out fears with faith (Hebrews 11:1-6).
15. Let go and let God take over. The only way to find peace and happiness is to let God take control of our life (Psalms 23).

Stories to Live By

The Card Room

In that place between wakefulness and dreams, I found myself in a room with no distinguishing features, except for one wall covered with small index card files. They were like the ones in the libraries that list titles by author or subject in alphabetical order. But these files, which stretched from floor to ceiling and seemed to stretch endlessly in either direction, had very different headings. As I drew near the wall of files, the first to catch my attention was one that read, "Girls I Have Liked." I opened it and began flipping through the cards. I quickly shut it, shocked to realize that I recognized the names written on each one.

And then, without being told, I knew exactly where I was. This lifeless room with its small files was a sophisticated catalog system for my life. Here were written the actions of my every moment, big and small, in a detail my memory couldn't match. A sense of wonder and curiosity, coupled with horror, stirred within me as I began randomly opening files and exploring their content. Some brought joy and sweet memories; others a sense of shame and regret so intense that I would look over my shoulder to see if anyone was watching. For example, a file named "Friends" was next to one marked "Friends I Have Betrayed."

The titles ranged from the mundane to the outright weird: "Books I Have Read," "Lies I Have Told," "Things I Have Done In My Anger," "Things I Have Muttered Under My Breath." I never ceased to be surprised by the contents. Often there were many more cards than I expected ... sometimes fewer than I hoped.

I was overwhelmed by the sheer volume of the life I had lived. Could it be possible that I had the time in my few years on earth to write each of these thousands or even millions of cards? But each card confirmed this truth. Each was written in my own handwriting and signed with my signature.

When I came to a file marked "Lustful Thoughts," I felt a chill run through my body. I pulled the file out only an inch, not willing to test its size, and drew out a card. I shuddered at its detailed content. I felt sick to think that such a moment had been recorded. An almost animal rage broke on me. One thought dominated my mind: "No one must ever see these cards! No one must ever see this room! I have to destroy them!" In an insane frenzy, I yanked the file out. Its size didn't matter now. I had to empty it and burn the cards. But as I took it at one end and began pounding it on the floor, I could not dislodge a single card. I became desperate and pulled out a card, only to find it as strong as steel when I tried to tear it.

Defeated and utterly helpless, I returned the file to its slot. Leaning my forehead against the wall, I let out a long, self-pitying sigh. And then I saw it. The title bore "People I Have Shared the Gospel With." The handle was brighter than those around it. Newer, almost unused. I pulled on its handle and a small box not more than three inches long fell into my hands. I could count the cards it contained on one hand.

And then the tears came. I began to weep, sobs so deep that the pain started in my stomach and shook through me. I fell on my knees and cried out in shame. The rows of shelved files swirled in my tear-filled eyes as I thought, "No one must ever, ever know of this room! I must lock it up and hide the key."

But then as I pushed away the tears, I saw Him. "No, please— not Him! Not here! Oh, anyone but Jesus." I watched helplessly as He began to open the files and read the cards. I couldn't bear to watch His response. And in the moments that I could bring my self to look at His face, I saw a sorrow deeper than my own. He seemed to intuitively go to the worst boxes. Why did He have to read every word?

Finally, He turned and looked at me from across the room with pity in His eyes. But this was a pity that didn't anger me. I slumped to the floor with my head drooped, covered my face with my hands, and again began to cry. He walked over and put His arms around me. He could have said so many things, but He didn't say a word. He just cried with me.

Then He got up and walked back to the wall of files. Starting at one end of the room, He took out each file and, one by one, began to sign His name over mine on each card.

"No," I shouted, rushing to Him. All I could find to say was "No! No!" as I pulled the card from Him. His name shouldn't be on these cards. But there it was, written in red ... So rich ... So dark ... So alive. The name of Jesus covered mine. It was written in His blood.

He gently took the card back and, smiling a sad smile, again began to sign the cards. I don't think I'll ever understand how He did it so quickly, but it seemed in the next instant I heard Him close the last file and walk back to my side. He placed His hand on my shoulder and said, "It is finished."

I stood up, and He led me out of the room. There was no lock on its door ... and there were still cards to be written.

The Old Mule

A parable is told of a farmer who owned an old mule. The mule fell into the farmer's well, and he heard the mule "braying," or whatever mules do when they fall into wells.

After carefully assessing the situation, the farmer sympathized with the mule, but decided that neither the mule nor the well was worth the trouble of saving. Instead, he called his neighbors together and told them what had happened and enlisted them to help haul dirt to bury the old mule in the well and put him out of his misery.

Initially, the old mule was hysterical! But as the farmer and his neighbors continued shoveling and the dirt hit his back, a thought struck him. Every time a shovel load of dirt landed on his back, *he should shake it off and step up!* This he did, blow after blow. "Shake it off and step up. Shake it off and step up. Shake it off and step up!" he repeated to encourage himself. No matter how painful the blows, or distressing the situation seemed, the old mule fought panic and just kept right on *shaking it off and stepping up!*

Well, you guessed it. It wasn't long before the old mule, battered and exhausted, stepped triumphantly over the wall of that well! What seemed like it would bury him, actually blessed him — all because of the manner in which he handled his adversity.

Hey, my friend, isn't that life? If we face our problems and respond to them positively, refusing to give in to panic, bitterness, or self-pity, the adversities that come along to bury us usually have within them the potential to benefit and bless us!

Remember that forgiveness, faith, prayer, praise, and hope are all excellent ways to "shake it off and step up" out of the wells in which we find ourselves!

The Deck of Cards

A group of soldiers in the North Africa Campaign in World War II returned to camp after heavy fighting.

The next day, Sunday, the Chaplain set up church service. The men were asked to take out their Bibles or Prayer Books. The Chaplain noticed one soldier looking at a deck of cards. After the service, he was taken by the Chaplain to see the Major.

The Chaplain explained to the Major what he had seen. The Major told the young soldier he would have to be punished if he could not explain himself.

The young soldier told the Major that during the battle, he had neither a Bible nor a Prayer Book, so he would use his deck of cards.

He explained: "You see, Sir, when I look at the *ace*, it tells me that there is one *God* and no other.

"When I see the '2,' it reminds me that there are two parts to the Bible, the *Old Testament* and the *New Testament.*

"The '3' tells me of the *trinity of God—the Father, God the Son, and God the Holy Spirit.*

"The '4' reminds me of the *four gospels, Matthew, Mark, Luke, and John.*

"When I see the '5,' it tells me of the *five unwise virgins* who were lost and that five were saved.

"The '6' reminds me that *God created the earth in just six days,* and that *God* said that it was good.

"When I see the '7,' it reminds me that *God rested on the seventh day.*

"As I look at the '8,' it reminds me that *God destroyed all life by water except for eight people*—Noah, his wife, their three sons, and their three sons' wives.

"When I see the '9,' I think of *nine lepers* that *God* healed. There were ten lepers in all, but only one stopped to thank him.

"The '10', reminds me of the *Ten Commandments* carved in stone by the hand of God.

"The 'Jack' makes me remember the Prince of Darkness. Like a roaring lion, he devours those he can."

"When I look at the 'Queen,' I see the *Blessed Virgin Mary, Mother of Jesus.*

"As I look at the last card 'the King,' it reminds me that *Jesus is Lord of lords and King of kings!*

"There are 365 spots on a deck of cards—the number of days in each year.

"There are 52 cards to a deck—the number of weeks in a year.

"There are 12 picture cards—the number of months in a year.

"There are 4 different suits in a deck—the number of seasons in a year."

And so, the young soldier then said to the Major, "You see, Sir, that my intentions were honorable. My deck of cards serves as my *Bible, my Prayer Book, and my Almanac.*"

Most important, a deck of cards should remind us that we need *Jesus* 365 days, 52 weeks and 12 months a year and that we should always *pray* "4" others.

May you never look at a deck of cards the same way.

Tips for a Fuller Life

Eating & Drinking

For those of you who watch what you eat, here's the final word on nutrition and health. It's a relief to know the truth after all those conflicting medical studies.

1. The Japanese eat very little fat and suffer fewer heart attacks than the British or Americans.
2. The Mexicans eat a lot of fat and also suffer fewer heart attacks than the British or Americans.
3. The Japanese drink very little red wine and suffer fewer heart attacks than the British or Americans.
4. The Italians drink excessive amounts of red wine and also suffer fewer heart attacks than the British or Americans.
5. The Germans drink a lot of beer and eat lots of sausages and fats and suffer fewer heart attacks than the British or Americans.

CONCLUSION: Eat and drink what you like. Speaking English is apparently what kills you.

Thought You Might Like This

It doesn't interest me what you do for a living.
I want to know what you ache for, and if you dare to dream of meeting your heart's longing.

It doesn't interest me how old you are.
I want to know if you will risk looking like a fool for love, for your dreams, for the adventure of being alive.

It doesn't interest me what planets are squaring your moon.
I want to know if you have touched the center of your own sorrow, if you have been opened up by life's betrayals, or have become shriveled and closed from fear of further pain.
I want to know if you can sit with pain, mine or your own, without moving to hide it or fade it or fix it.
I want to know if you can dance with joy, mine or your own; if you dance with wildness and let the ecstasy fill you to the tips of your fingers and toes without cautioning us to be careful, be realistic, or to remember the limitations of being human.

It doesn't interest me if the story you're telling me is true.
I want to know if you can disappoint another to be true to yourself. If you can bare the accusation of betrayal and not betray your own soul.
I want to know if you can be faithful, and therefore be trustworthy.
I want to know if you can see beauty even when it is not pretty every day, and if you can source your life from God's presence.

I want to know if you can live with failure, mine and yours, and still stand on the edge of a lake and shout, "YES!" to the light of the full moon.

It doesn't interest me who you are or how you came to be here. I want to know if you will stand in the center of the fire with me and not shrink back.

It doesn't interest me where or what or with whom you have studied.

I want to know what sustains you from the inside when all else falls away.

I want to know if you can be alone with yourself.

And if you truly like the company you keep in the empty moments.

(Oriah Mountain Dreamer, Indian Elder)

Three Things

Three things in life that, once gone, never come back:
Time
Words
Opportunity

Three things in life that may never be lost:
Peace
Hope
Honesty

Three things in life that are most valuable:
Love
Self-confidence
Friends

Three things in life that are never certain:
Dreams
Success
Fortune

Three things that make a man:
Hard work
Sincerity
Commitment

Three things in life that can destroy a man:
Wine
Pride
Anger

Three things that are truly constant:
Father
Son
Holy Ghost

I ask the Lord to bless you, as I pray for you today, to guide you and protect you, as you go along your way. His love is always with you; His promises are true. And when you give Him all your cares, you know He'll see you through.

Access
Amazing Stories

10

The Value of a Window

Windows into the Soul
The Weathered Old Barn
Don't Ever Give Up on Your Dream
The Quarter
Why Go to Church?

Stories of Incredible Faith
Twinkies and Root Beer
Words from Lincoln
The Scales

Miracles of Love
God's Wings
Priceless Glass of Milk
A Sandpiper to Bring You Joy
Rudy Angel

Science Speaks God's Language
NASA Uses the Bible
The Human Mind

Kindness Conquers
The Living Bible

Mark's Treasure

God Is Still There
The World Came Together

God's Positive Answers

The Butterfly

Running the Race

A Neat Love Story

Who's Your Daddy?

"Let's Roll": The Faith of Todd Beamer

The Value of a Window

When Carolyn put her house up for sale, she changed the window treatments in her living room. The huge picture window had long, heavy drapes covering them because they matched the décor of Carolyn's antique furniture. But now Carolyn wanted to emphasize the view from the picture window. It overlooked a perfectly groomed back yard, which led to the foothills of the grand Rocky Mountains. The view looked like the photos on picture puzzles for sale in the drug store. Carolyn knew that the view would enhance the sale of her house.

If Carolyn's window had faced the sight of a busy freeway, she would have had a far different idea of what window treatments to use. Then she would have wanted window treatments that covered up the view.

Have you ever thought of what people would see if you had a picture window on your soul? We have many things hidden deep within us that we don't share with anyone else. And these secret parts of our soul aren't necessary skeletons in the closet. Sometimes we are surprised by the goodness and compassion that we find within ourselves.

What if you could view the soul of your friend or a stranger on the street? What would you see? Perhaps you would find that the person you consider your best friend has a deeper love for you than you expected. Perhaps you would see the jewel-like beauty of a stranger's heart.

In the newspaper and on the broadcast news, we constantly hear about the evils of mankind—the murders, the greed, the hate. We don't often hear about the wonderful stories of self-sacrifice and selflessness that go on in our world every day.

These stories will warm your heart as you get a glimpse into the souls of everyday people who do extraordinary things.

• The little boy who meets God
• The wisdom and compassion of Mother Teresa
• The woman who was generous when it was inconvenient
• The faith of Todd Beamer, who confronted terrorists on a plane

Each of these stories and poems is an experience in itself. Read through them as if you were on a journey, stopping to view the scenery and historical points along the way. When you read each one, someone's name may come to mind. "Oh, Jennifer would love reading this one. This is just where she's at in her life," or "This story would encourage James. He needs to read this one."

Then share the best ones with your friends. See what their reactions are. The entries in this chapter will provide you with many encouraging messages for your friends and may open the window on a soul that will surprise and delight you.

Windows into the Soul

The Weathered Old Barn

A stranger came by the other day with an offer that set me to thinking. He wanted to buy the old barn that sits out by the highway. I told him right off he was crazy. He was a city type. You could tell by his clothes, his car, his hands, and the way he talked.

He said he was driving by and saw that beautiful barn sitting out in the tall grass and wanted to know if it was for sale. I told him he had a funny idea of beauty. Sure, it was a handsome building in its day, but then, there's been a lot of winters pass with their snow, ice and howling wind. The summer sun's beat down on that ole' barn till all the paint's gone, and the wood has turned silver gray. Now the old building leans a good deal and is looking kind of tired. Yet, that fellow called it beautiful.

That set me to thinking. I walked out to the field and just stood there, gazing at that old barn. The stranger said he planned to use the lumber to line the walls of his den in a new country home he's building down the road. He said you couldn't get paint that beautiful. Only years of standing in the weather, bearing the storms and scorching sun ... only that can produce beautiful barn wood.

It came to me then. We're a lot like that, you and I. Only it's on the inside that the beauty grows with us. Sure, we turn silver gray, too ... and lean a bit more than we did when we were young and full of sap. But the Good Lord knows what He's doing. And as the years pass, He's busy using the hard wealth of our lives, the dry spells and the stormy seasons, to do a job of beautifying our souls that nothing else can produce. And to think how often folks holler because they want life easy!

They took the old barn down today and hauled it away to beautify a rich man's house. And I reckon someday you and I'll be hauled off to Heaven to take on whatever chores the Good Lord has for us on the Great Sky Ranch. And I suspect we'll be more beautiful then for the seasons we've been through here ... and just maybe even add a bit of beauty to our Father's house.

(Gordon Knapp)

Don't Ever Give Up On Your Dream

He failed in business in '31.
He was defeated for state legislator in '32.
He tried another business in '33.
It failed.

His fiancee died in '35.
He had a nervous breakdown in '36.
In '43, he ran for Congress and was defeated.
He tried again in '48 and was defeated again.
He tried running for the Senate in '55.
He lost.

The next year he ran for Vice President and lost.
In '59, he ran for the Senate again and was defeated.
In 1860, this man was elected the 16th President of the United States. He was the first Republican to be elected President. His name—Abraham Lincoln.

The difference between history's boldest accomplishments and its most staggering failures is often simply the diligent will to persevere.

The Quarter

Several years ago, a preacher moved to Houston, Texas. Some weeks after he arrived, he had occasion to ride a bus from his home to the downtown area. When he sat down, he discovered that the driver had accidentally given him a quarter too much change. As he considered what to do, he thought to himself, "I'd better give the quarter back. It would be wrong to keep it."

Then he thought, "Oh, forget it, it's only a quarter. Who would worry about this little amount? Anyway, the bus company already gets too much fare; they will never miss it. Accept it as a gift from God and keep quiet."

When his stop came, he paused momentarily at the door, then he handed the quarter to the driver and said, "Here, you gave me too much change."

With a smile, the driver replied, "Aren't you the new preacher in town? I have been thinking lately about going to worship somewhere. I just wanted to see what you would do if I gave you too much change."

When my friend stepped off the bus, he literally grabbed the nearest light pole, held on, and said, "O God, I almost sold Your Son for a quarter."

Our lives are the only Bible some people will ever read. With God all things are possible (Matthew 19:26).

Why Go to Church?

A churchgoer wrote a letter to the editor of the newspaper and complained that it made no sense to go to church every Sunday. "I've gone for 30 years now," he wrote, "and in that time I have heard something like 3,000 sermons. But for the life of me, I can't remember a single one of them. So, I think I'm wasting my time, and the pastors are wasting theirs by giving sermons at all."

This started a real controversy in the "Letters to the Editor" column, much to the delight of the editor. It went on for weeks until someone wrote this clincher:

"I've been married for 30 years now. In that time, my wife has cooked some 32,000 meals. But for the life of me, I cannot recall the entire menu for a single one of those meals. But I do know this: They all nourished me and gave me the strength I needed to do my work. If my wife had not given me those meals, I would be physically dead today. Likewise, if I had not gone to church for nourishment, I would be spiritually dead today!"

When you are DOWN to nothing, God is UP to something! Faith sees the invisible, believes the incredible, and receives the impossible! Thank God for our physical *and* our spiritual nourishment!

Stories of Incredible Faith

Twinkies and Root Beer

A little boy wanted to meet God. He knew it was a long trip to where God lived, so he packed his suitcase with Twinkies, a six-pack of root beer, and he started his journey. When he had gone about three blocks, he met an old man who was sitting in the park just staring at some pigeons. The boy sat down next to him and opened his suitcase. He was about to take a drink from his root beer when he noticed that the old man looked hungry, so he offered him a Twinkie.

The old man gratefully accepted it and smiled at him. His smile was so pleasant that the boy wanted to see it again, so he offered him a root beer. Again, he smiled at him. The boy was delighted! They sat there all afternoon eating and smiling, but they never said a word.

As it grew dark, the boy realized how tired he was, so he got up to leave. But before he had gone more than a few steps, he turned around, ran back to the old man, and gave him a hug. He gave him his biggest smile ever.

When the boy opened the door to his own house a short time later, his mother was surprised by the look of joy on his face. She asked him, "What did you do today that made you so happy?"

He replied, "I had lunch with God." But before his mother could respond, he added, "You know what? He's got the most beautiful smile I've ever seen!"

Meanwhile, the old man, also radiant with joy, returned to his home. His son was stunned by the look of peace on his face and asked, "Dad, what did you do today that made you so happy?"

He replied, "I ate Twinkies in the park with God." However, before his son responded, he added, "You know, He's much younger than I expected."

Too often we underestimate the power of a touch, a smile, a kind word, a listening ear, an honest compliment, or the smallest act of caring, all of which have the potential to turn a life around. People come into our lives for a reason, a season, or a lifetime. Embrace all equally!

Words from Lincoln

This is a little known conversation between General Horatio King and President Lincoln.

"Are you a Christian? Do you love the Lord Jesus Christ?" asked King.

The President slowly replied, "When I left Springfield, I asked the people to pray for me. I was not a Christian. When I buried my son, the severest trial of my life, I was not a Christian. But when I went to Gettysburg and saw the graves of thousands of soldiers, I then and there consecrated myself to Christ. Yes, General, I do love Jesus."

The Scales

Louise Redden, a poorly dressed lady with a look of defeat on her face, walked into a grocery store. She approached the owner of the store in a most humble manner and asked if he would let her charge a few groceries. She softly explained that her husband was very ill and unable to work; they had seven children and they needed food.

John Longhouse, the grocer, scoffed at her and requested she leave his store.

Visualizing the family needs, she said, "Please, sir! I will bring you the money just as soon as I can."

John told her he could not give her credit because she did not have a charge account at his store.

Standing beside the counter was a customer who overheard the conversation between the two. The customer walked forward and told the grocer that he would stand good for whatever she needed for her family.

The grocer said in a very reluctant voice, "Do you have a grocery list?"

Louise replied, "Yes sir!"

"OK," he said, "Put your grocery list on the scales, and whatever your grocery list weighs, I will give you that amount in groceries."

Louise hesitated a moment with a bowed head, then she reached into her purse and took out a piece of paper and scribbled something on it. She then carefully laid the piece of paper on the scale with her head still bowed. The eyes of the grocer and the customer showed amazement when the scales went down and stayed down.

The grocer, staring at the scales, turned slowly to the customer and said begrudgingly, "I can't believe it."

The customer smiled, and the grocer started putting the groceries on the other side of the scales. The scale did not balance, so he continued to put more and more groceries on them until the scales would hold no more. The grocer stood there in utter disgust. Finally, he grabbed the piece of paper from the scales and looked at it with even greater amazement.

It was not a grocery list, it was a prayer, which said: "Dear Lord, you know my needs and I am leaving this in your hands." The grocer gave her the groceries he gathered from the scales and stood in stunned silence. Louise thanked him and left the store.

The customer handed a fifty-dollar bill to John as he said, "It was worth every penny of it."

It was sometime later that John Longhouse discovered the scales were broken, therefore only God knows how much a prayer weighs.

Miracles of Love

God's Wings

An article in *National Geographic* several years ago provided a penetrating picture of God's wings. After a forest fire in Yellowstone National Park, forest rangers began their trek up a mountain to assess the inferno's damage.

One ranger found a bird literally petrified in ashes, perched statuesquely on the ground at the base of a tree. Somewhat sickened by the eerie sight, he knocked over the bird with a stick. When he gently struck it, three tiny chicks scurried from under their dead mother's wings.

The loving mother, keenly aware of impending disaster, had carried her offspring to the base of the tree and had gathered them under her wings, instinctively knowing that the toxic smoke would rise. She could have flown to safety but had refused to abandon her babies. When the blaze had arrived and the heat had scorched her small body, the mother had remained steadfast. Because she had been willing to die, those under the cover of her wings would live.

"He will cover you with feathers, and under his wings you will find refuge" (Psalm 91:4).

Being loved this much should make a difference in your life. Remember the one who loves you and then be different because of it.

Priceless Glass of Milk

One day, a poor boy, who was selling goods from door to door to pay his way through school, found that he had only one thin dime left, and he was hungry. He decided he would ask for a meal at the next house. However, he lost his nerve when a lovely young woman opened the door. Instead of a meal, he asked for a drink of water. She thought he looked hungry, so she brought him a large glass of milk.

He drank it slowly, then asked, "How much do I owe you?"

"You don't owe me anything," she replied.

"Mother taught us never to accept pay for a kindness," she said.

"Then I thank you from my heart."

As Howard Kelly left that house, he not only felt stronger physically, but his faith in God and man was strong also. He had been ready to give up and quit.

Years later, that young woman became critically ill. The local doctors were baffled. They finally sent her to the big city where they called in specialists to study her rare disease. Dr. Howard Kelly was called in for the consultation. When he heard the name of the town she came from, a strange light filled his eyes. Immediately, he rose and went down the hall of the hospital to her room. Dressed in his doctor's gown, he went in to see her, and he recognized her at once. He went back to the consultation room determined to do his best to save her life.

From that day, he gave special attention to the case. After a long struggle, the battle was won. Dr. Kelly requested the business office to pass the final bill to him for approval. He looked at it, then wrote something on the edge, and it was sent to her room. She feared to open it because she was sure it would take the rest of her life to pay for it all. Finally, she looked, and something caught her attention on the side of the bill. She read these words, "Paid in full with one glass of milk."

Under the sentence was a signature: Dr. Howard Kelly

Tears of joy flooded her eyes as her happy heart prayed, "Thank You, God. Your love has spread abroad through human hearts and hands."

A Sandpiper to Bring You Joy

She was six years old when I first met her on the beach near where I live. I drive to this beach, a distance of three or four miles, whenever the world begins to close in on me. She was building a sandcastle or something and looked up, her eyes as blue as the sea.

"Hello," she said.

I answered with a nod, not really in the mood to bother with a small child.

"I'm building," she said.

"I see that. What is it?" I asked, not caring.

"Oh, I don't know, I just like the feel of sand."

That sounds good, I thought, and slipped off my shoes.

A sandpiper glided by.

"That's a joy," the child said.

"It's a what?"

"It's a joy. My mama says sandpipers come to bring us joy."

The bird went gliding down the beach.

"Good-bye, joy," I muttered to myself, "Hello, pain," and turned to walk on. I was depressed; my life seemed completely out of balance.

"What's your name?" She wouldn't give up.

"Robert," I answered. "I'm Robert Peterson."

"Mine's Wendy. I'm six."

"Hi, Wendy."

She giggled. "You're funny."

In spite of my gloom, I laughed too and walked on. Her musical giggle followed me.

"Come again, Mr. P," she called. "We'll have another happy day."

The days and weeks that followed belonged to others: a group of unruly Boy Scouts, PTA meetings, and an ailing mother. The sun was shining one morning as I took my hands out of the dishwater. "I need a sandpiper," I said to myself, gathering up my coat.

The ever-changing balm of the seashore awaited me. The breeze was chilly, but I strode along, trying to recapture the serenity I needed. I had forgotten the child and was startled when she appeared.

"Hello, Mr. P," she said. "Do you want to play?"

"What did you have in mind?" I asked with a twinge of annoyance.

"I don't know. You say."

"How about charades?" I asked sarcastically.

The tinkling laughter burst forth again. "I don't know what that is."

"Then let's just walk." Looking at her, I noticed the delicate fairness of her face. "Where do you live?" I asked.

"Over there." She pointed toward a row of summer cottages. *Strange,* I thought, *it's winter.* "Where do you go to school?" I asked.

"I don't go to school. Mommy says we're on vacation."

She chattered little-girl talk as we strolled up the beach, but my mind was on other things. When I left for home, Wendy said it had been a happy day. Feeling surprisingly better, I smiled at her and agreed.

Three weeks later, I rushed to my beach in a state of near panic. I was in no mood to even greet Wendy. I thought I saw her mother on the porch and felt like demanding she keep her child at home. "Look, if you don't mind," I said crossly when Wendy caught up with me, "I'd rather be alone today."

She seemed unusually pale and out of breath. "Why?" she asked.

I turned to her and shouted, "Because my mother died!" and thought, *My God, why was I saying this to a little child?*

"Oh," she said quietly, "then this is a bad day."

"Yes," I said "and yesterday and the day before and—oh, go away!"

"Did it hurt?" she inquired.

"Did what hurt?" I was exasperated with her, with myself.

"When she died?"

"Of course it hurt!" I snapped, misunderstanding, wrapped up in myself. I strode off.

A month or so after that when I next went to the beach, she wasn't there. Feeling guilty, ashamed, and admitting to myself that I missed her, I went up to the cottage after my walk and knocked at the door. A drawn-looking young woman with honey-colored hair opened the door.

"Hello," I said. "I'm Robert Peterson. I missed your little girl today and wondered where she was."

"Oh yes, Mr. Peterson, please come in. Wendy spoke of you so much. I'm afraid I allowed her to bother you. If she was a nuisance, please, accept my apologies."

"Not at all. She's a delightful child," I said, suddenly realizing that I meant what I had just said.

"Wendy died last week, Mr. Peterson. She had leukemia. Maybe she didn't tell you."

Struck dumb, I groped for a chair. I had to catch my breath.

"She loved this beach, so when she asked to come, we couldn't say no. She seemed so much better here and had a lot of what she called happy days. But the last few weeks, she declined rapidly ..." Her voice faltered, "She left something for you ... if only I could find it. Could you wait a minute while I look?"

I nodded stupidly, my mind racing for something to say to this lovely young woman. She handed me a smeared envelope with MR. P printed in bold, childish letters. Inside was a drawing in bright crayon hues—a yellow beach, a blue sea, and a brown bird.

Underneath was carefully printed: A SANDPIPER TO BRING YOU JOY.

Tears welled up in my eyes and a heart that had almost forgotten to love opened wide. I took Wendy's mother in my arms. "I'm so sorry, I'm so sorry, I'm so sorry," I muttered over and over, and we wept together.

The precious little picture is framed now and hangs in my study. Six words—one for each year of her life—speak to me of harmony, courage, and undemanding love. A gift from a child with sea-blue eyes and hair the color of sand—who taught me the gift of love.

NOTE: This is a true story sent in by Robert Peterson. It serves as a reminder to all of us that we need to take time to enjoy living and life and each other. Be sure to give your loved ones an extra hug, and by all means, take a moment—even if it is only ten seconds—to stop and smell the roses.

Rudy Angel

I walked into the grocery store not particularly interested in buying groceries. I wasn't hungry.

The pain of losing my husband of 37 years was still too raw. And this grocery store held so many sweet memories. Rudy often came with me, and almost every time he'd pretend to go off and look for something special. I always knew what he was up to and would spot him walking down the aisle with three yellow roses in his hands.

Rudy knew I loved yellow roses. With a heart filled with grief, I only wanted to buy my few items and leave, but even grocery shopping was different since Rudy had passed on.

Shopping for one took a little more time and thought than it had for two. Standing by the meat, I searched for the perfect small steak and remembered how Rudy had loved his steak.

Suddenly, a woman came beside me. She was blond, slim, and lovely in a soft green pantsuit. I watched as she picked up a large pack of T-bones, dropped them in her basket, hesitated, and then put them back. She turned to go, then once again reached for the pack of steaks. When she saw me watching her, she smiled. "My husband loves T-bones, but honestly, at these prices, I don't know."

I swallowed the emotion and met her pale blue eyes. "My husband passed away eight days ago," I told her. Glancing at the package in her hands, I fought to control the tremble in my voice. "Buy him the steaks. And cherish every moment you have together."

She shook her head, and I saw the emotion in her eyes as she placed the package in her basket and wheeled away. I turned and pushed my cart across the length of the store to the dairy products. There I stood, trying to decide which size milk I should buy. *A quart*, I finally decided and moved on to the ice cream section near the front of the store. If nothing else, I could always fix myself an ice cream cone.

I placed the ice cream in my cart and looked down the aisle toward the front of the store. First, I saw the green suit, then recognized the pretty lady coming towards me. In her arms, she carried a package. On her face was the brightest smile I had ever seen. I would swear a soft halo encircled her blond hair as she kept walking toward me, her eyes holding mine. As she came closer, I saw what she held, and tears began misting in my eyes.

"These are for you," she said and placed three beautiful long-stemmed yellow roses in my arms. "When you go through the line, they will know these are paid for." She leaned over and placed a gentle kiss on my check, then smiled again.

I wanted to tell her what she'd done, what the roses meant, but was unable to speak. I watched her walk away as tears clouded my vision. I looked down at the beautiful roses nestled in the green tissue wrapping and found it almost unreal. How did she know?

Suddenly, the answer seemed so clear. I wasn't alone. "Oh, Rudy, you haven't forgotten me, have you?" I whispered. He was still with me, and she was his angel.

Every day be thankful for what you have and who you are.

Science Speaks God's Language

NASA Uses the Bible

For all you scientists out there and all the students who have a hard time convincing these people regarding the truth of the Bible, here's something that shows God's awesome creation and shows that He is still in control. Did you know that the space program is busy proving that what has been called "myth" in the Bible is true? Mr. Harold Hill, President of the Curtis Engine Co. in Baltimore, Maryland, and a consultant in the space program, relates the following development:

I think one of the most amazing things that God has for us today happened recently to our astronauts and space scientists at Greenbelt, Maryland. They were checking the position of the sun, moon, and planets out in space where they would be 100 years and 1,000 years from now. We have to know this so that we won't send a satellite up and have it bump into something in its orbit later. We have to lay out the orbit in terms of the life of the satellite and where the planets will be so the whole thing will not bog down.

The scientists ran the computer measurement back and forth over the centuries, and it came to a halt. The computer stopped and put out a red signal, which meant that there was something wrong either with the information fed into it or with the results as compared to the standards. They called in the service department to check it out. Well, they found that there is a day missing in space in elapsed time. They scratched their heads and tore their hair. There was no answer. Finally, a Christian man on the team said, "You know, one time I was in Sunday school, and the teacher talked about the sun standing still."

While the others didn't believe him, they didn't have an answer either, so they said, "Show us."

He got a Bible and went back to the Book of Joshua where they found a pretty ridiculous statement for any one with "common sense." The Lord says to Joshua, "Fear them not, I have delivered them into thy hand; there shall not a man of them stand before thee." Joshua was concerned because he and his army were surrounded by the enemy and if darkness fell their enemies would overpower them. So, Joshua asked the Lord to make the sun stand still! That's right! "The sun stood still and the moon stayed—and hastened not to go down about a whole day!"

The astronauts and scientists said, "There is the missing day!" They checked the computers going back into the time when the account was written. They found it was close, but not close enough. The elapsed time that was missing back in Joshua's day was 23 hours and 20 minutes—not a whole day.

They read in the Bible that the time was "about (approximately) a day." These little words in the Bible are important. But the scientists were still in trouble if they could not account for the missing forty minutes, and the satellite would still be in trouble 1,000 years from now. Forty minutes had to be found because it can be multiplied many times over in orbits.

As the Christian employee thought about it, he remembered somewhere in the Bible where it said the sun went *backwards*.

The scientist told him he was out of his mind, but they got out the Book and read these words in 2 Kings: Hezekiah, on his deathbed, was visited by the prophet Isaiah who told him that he was not going to die. Hezekiah asked for a sign as proof. Isaiah said, "Do you want the sun to go ahead 10 degrees?"

Hezekiah said "It is nothing for the sun to go ahead 10 degrees, let the shadow return backward 10 degrees." Isaiah spoke to the Lord and the Lord brought the shadow ten degrees *backwards*! Ten degrees is exactly 40 minutes! Twenty-three hours and 20 minutes in Joshua, plus 40 minutes in 2 Kings, make up the missing day in the universe!

Isn't it amazing? Our God is so awesome!

References: Joshua 10:8, 12, 13, and 2 Kings 20:9-11

The Human Mind

An interesting thing about the human mind ...

I cdnuolt blveiee taht I cluod aulaclty uesdnatnrd waht I was rdanieg.

The phaonmneal pweor of the hmuan mnid.

Aoccdrnig to a rscheearch at Cmabrigde Uinervtisy, it deosn't mttaer in waht oredr the ltteers in a wrod are, the olny iprmoatnt tihng is that the frist and lsat ltteer be in the rghit pclae.

The rset can be a taotl mses and you can sitll raed it wouthit a porbelm. Tihs is bcuseae the huamn mnid deos not raed ervey lteter by istlef, but the wrod as a wlohe. Amzanig huh? Yaeh and I awlyas thought slpeling was ipmorantt.

And who can believe that this phenomenal organ—the human mind—was evolved by chance? Only God could have created such a miraculous and efficient thing!

Kindness Conquers

The Living Bible

His name is Bill. He has wild hair, wears a T-shirt with holes in it, jeans, and no shoes. This had been his wardrobe for his entire four years of college. He is brilliant, kind of esoteric, and very, very bright. He became a Christian while attending college.

Across the street from the campus is a well-dressed, very conservative church. They want to develop a ministry to the students, but are not sure how to go about it. One day, Bill decides to go there. He walks in with no shoes, jeans, his T-shirt, and wild hair. The service had already started, so Bill starts down the aisle looking for a seat. The church is completely packed, and he can't find a seat. By now, people are looking a bit uncomfortable, but no one says anything.

Bill gets closer, and closer, and closer to the pulpit, and when he realizes there are no seats, he just squats down right on the carpet. (Although perfectly acceptable behavior at a college fellowship, trust me, this has never happened in this church before!) By now, the people are really uptight, and the tension in the air is thick.

About this time, the minister realizes that from way at the back of the church, a deacon is slowly making his way toward Bill. The deacon is in his eighties, has silver-gray hair, and is wearing a three-piece suit. He is a godly man, very elegant, very dignified, very courtly.

He uses a cane, and as he starts walking toward this boy, everyone is saying to himself, "You can't blame him for what he's going to do. How can you expect a man of his age and of his background to understand some college kid on the floor?"

It takes a long time for the man to walk to the front. The church is utterly silent except for the clicking of the man's cane. All eyes are focused on him. You can't even hear anyone breathing. The minister can't continue preaching the sermon until the deacon does what he has to do.

Then this elderly man drops his cane on the floor. With great difficulty, he lowers himself, sits down next to Bil, and worships with him so that he won't be alone.

Everyone chokes up with emotion. When the minister gains control, he says, "What I'm about to preach, you will never remember. What you have just seen, you will never forget. Be careful how you live. You may be the only Bible some people will ever read."

Lord, help me to be as accepting of others as you are of me. You accept me no matter how I am dressed or what I have done. Open my heart to accept others as quickly and fully in love! Lord, like You forgave my sins , help me forgive other's sins against me. Help me to become more like Christ. In Jesus' name I pray, Amen.

Mark's Treasure

He was in the first third-grade class that I taught at Saint Mary's School in Morris, Minnesota. All 34 of my students were dear to me, but Mark Eklund was one in a million. Very neat in appearance, he had that happy-to-be-alive attitude that made even his occasional mischievous acts delightful.

Mark talked incessantly. I had to remind him again and again that talking without permission was not acceptable. What impressed me so much, though, was his sincere response every time I had to correct him for misbehaving. "Thank you for correcting me, Sister!" I didn't know what to make of his response at first, but before long, I became accustomed to hearing it many times a day.

One morning my patience was growing thin when Mark talked once too often, and then I made a novice teacher's mistake. I looked at Mark and said, "If you say one more word, I am going to tape your mouth shut!"

It wasn't ten seconds later when Chuck blurted out, "Mark is talking again."

I hadn't asked any of the students to help me watch Mark, but since I had stated the punishment in front of the class, I had to act on it. I remember the scene as if it had occurred this morning. I walked to my desk, deliberately opened my drawer, and took out a roll of masking tape.

Without saying a word, I proceeded to Mark's desk, tore off two pieces of tape, and made a big X with them over his mouth. I then returned to the front of the room.

As I glanced at Mark to see how he was doing, he winked at me. That did it!! I started laughing. The class cheered as I walked back to Mark's desk, removed the tape, and shrugged my shoulders. His first words were, "Thank you for correcting me, Sister."

At the end of the year, I was asked to teach junior-high math. The years flew by, and before I knew it, Mark was in my classroom again. He was more handsome than ever and just as polite. Since he had to listen carefully to my instruction in "new math," he did not talk as much in ninth grade as he had in third.

One Friday, things just didn't feel right. We had worked hard on a new concept all week, and the students were frowning, frustrated with themselves and edgy with one another. I had to stop this crankiness before it got out of hand, so I asked them to list the names of the other students in the room on two sheets of paper, leaving a space between each name. Then I told them to think of the nicest thing they could say about each of their classmates and write it down. It took the remainder of the class period for the students to finish their assignment, and as the students left the room, each one handed me the papers.

Charlie smiled. Mark said, "Thank you for teaching me, Sister. Have a good weekend."

That Saturday, I wrote down the names of each student on a separate sheet of paper, and I listed what everyone else had said about that individual. On Monday, I gave each student his or her list. Before long, the entire class was smiling. "Really?" I heard whispered. "I never knew that meant anything to anyone!" "I didn't know others liked me so much." No one ever mentioned those papers in class again. I never knew if they discussed them after class or with their parents, but it did not matter. The exercise had accomplished its purpose. The students were happy with themselves and each other again.

That group of students moved on. Several years later, after I returned from vacation, my parents met me at the airport. As we were driving home, Mother asked me the usual questions about the trip—the weather, my experiences in general. There was a lull in the conversation. Mother gave Dad a sideways glance and simply said, "Dad?"

My father cleared his throat as he usually did before something important. "The Eklunds called last night," he began.

"Really?" I said. "I haven't heard from them in years. I wonder how Mark is doing."

Dad responded quietly. "Mark was killed in Vietnam," he said. "The funeral is tomorrow, and his parents would like it if you could attend."

To this day, I can still point the exact spot on I-494 where Dad told me about Mark.

I had never seen a serviceman in a military coffin before. Mark looked so handsome, so mature. All I could think at that moment was, *Mark, I would give all the masking tape in the world if only you would talk to me.*

The church was packed with Mark's friends. Chuck's sister sang *The Battle Hymn of the Republic.* Why did it have to rain on the day of the funeral? It was difficult enough at the graveside. The pastor said the usual prayers, and the bugler played "Taps." One by one, those who loved Mark took a last walk by the coffin and sprinkled it with holy water. I was the last one to bless the coffin.

As I stood there, one of the soldiers who acted as pallbearer came up to me. "Were you Mark's math teacher?" he asked.

I nodded as I continued to stare at the coffin.

"Mark talked about you a lot," he said.

After the funeral, most of Mark's former classmates headed to Chuck's farmhouse for lunch. Mark's mother and father were there, obviously waiting for me. "We want to show you something," his father said, taking a wallet out of his pocket. "They found this on Mark when he was killed. We thought you might recognize it."

Opening the billfold, he carefully removed two torn pieces of notebook paper that had obviously been taped, folded, and refolded many times. I knew without looking that the papers were the ones on which I had listed all the good things each of Mark's classmates had said about him.

"Thank you so much for doing that," Mark's mother said. "As you can see, Mark treasured it."

Mark's classmates started to gather around us.

Charlie smiled rather sheepishly and said, "I still have mine. It's in the top drawer of my desk at home."

Chuck's wife said, "Chuck asked me to put his in our wedding album."

"I have mine too," Marilyn said. "It's in my diary."

Then Vicki, another classmate, reached into her pocketbook, took out her wallet, and showed her worn and frazzled list to the group. "I carry this with me at all times," Vicki said without batting an eyelash. "I think we all saved our lists."

That's when I finally sat down and cried. I cried for Mark and for all his friends who would never see him again.

The density of people in society is so thick that we forget that life will end one day. And we don't know when that one day will be. So please, tell the people you love and care for that they are special and important. Tell them before it is too late.

God is Still There

The World Came Together

A father wanted to read a magazine, but was being bothered by his little daughter, Vanessa. Finally, he tore a sheet out of his magazine on which was printed the map of the world. Tearing it into small pieces, he gave it to Vanessa, and said, "Go into the other room and see if you can put this together."

After a few minutes, Vanessa returned and handed him the map correctly fitted together. The father was surprised and asked how she had finished so quickly.

"Oh," she said, "on the other side of the paper is a picture of Jesus. When I got all of Jesus back where He belonged, then the world came together."

God's Positive Answers

For all the negative things we have to say to ourselves, God has a positive answer for it.

You say: "It's impossible."

God says: "All things are possible" (Luke 18:27).

You say: "I'm too tired."

God says: "I will give you rest" (Matthew 11:18-20).

You say: "Nobody really loves me."

God says: "I love you" (John 3:16; John 13:34).

You say: "I can't go on."

God says: "My grace is sufficient" (2 Corinthians. 12:9; Psalm 91:15).

You say: "I can't figure things out."

God says: "I will direct your steps" (Proverbs 3:5,6).

You say: "I can't do it!"

God says: "You can do all things" (Philippians 4:13).

You say: "I'm not able."

God says: "I am able" (2 Corinthians 9:8).

You say: "It's not worth it."

God says: "It will be worth it" (Romans 8:28).

You say: "I can't forgive myself."

God says: "I forgive you" (I John 1:9; Romans 8:1).

You say: "I can't manage."

God says: "I will supply all your needs" (Philippians 4:19).

You say: "I'm afraid."

God says: "I have not given you a spirit of fear" (2 Timothy 1:7).

You say: "I'm always worried and frustrated."

God says: "Cast all your cares on me" (1 Peter 5:7).

You say: "I don't have enough faith."

God says: "I've given everyone a measure of faith" (Romans 12:3).

You say: "I'm not smart enough."

God says: "I give you wisdom" (1 Corinthians 1:30).

You say: "I feel all alone."

God says: "I will never leave you or forsake you" (Hebrews 13:5).

The Butterfly

A man found a cocoon of a butterfly. One day, a small opening appeared. He sat and watched the butterfly for several hours as it struggled to force its body through that little hole. Then it seemed to stop making any progress. It appeared as if it had gotten as far as it could and that it could go no further, so the man decided to help the butterfly. He took a pair of scissors and snipped off the remaining bit of the cocoon.

The butterfly then emerged easily. But it had a swollen body and small, shriveled wings.

The man continued to watch the butterfly because he expected that, at any moment, the wings would enlarge and expand and be able to support the body, which would contract in time. Neither happened! In fact, the butterfly spent the rest of its life crawling around with a swollen body and shriveled wings. It never was able to fly. What the man, in his kindness and haste, did not understand was that the restricting cocoon and the struggle required for the butterfly to get through the tiny opening was God's way of forcing fluid from the body of the butterfly into its wings so that it would be ready for flight once it achieved its freedom from the cocoon.

Sometimes struggles are exactly what we need in our lives. If God allowed us to go through our lives without any obstacles, we would be crippled. We would not be as strong as what we could have been. We could never fly!

Running the Race

In the 1992 Olympics, runner Derek Redmond competed in the 400-meter event. Unfortunately, he went down with a torn right hamstring on the backstretch. In excruciating pain, Redmond desperately tried to finish the race.

When he reached the final stretch, Derek's father ran out to the track to meet his son and said, "Son, we're going to finish this together!"

And they did. The son's head was sometimes buried on his father's shoulder, but they stayed in Derek's lane to the end as the crowd stood, cheered, and wept.

Do you feel like you are running by yourself? The Lord Jesus has already finished the race in first place. Now He's running with you to help you make it to the end. Whenever you feel like stopping, He's there to remind you, "We're going to finish this together."

A Neat Love Story

One day, I woke early in the morning to watch the sunrise, because the beauty of God's creation is beyond description. As I watched, I praised God for His beautiful work. Sitting there, I felt the Lord's presence with me.

He asked me, "Do you love Me?"

I answered, "Of course, God! You are my Lord and Savior!"

Then He asked, "If you were physically handicapped, would you still love Me?"

I was perplexed. I looked down upon my arms, legs, and the rest of my body and wondered how many things I wouldn't be able to do, the things that I took for granted. And I answered, "It would be tough Lord, but I would still love You."

Then the Lord said, "If you were blind, would you still love My creation?"

How could I love something without being able to see it? Then I thought of all the blind people in the world and how many of them still loved God and His creation. So I answered, "It's hard to think of it, but I would still love You."

Then the Lord asked me, "If you were deaf, would you still listen to My Word?"

How could I listen to anything being deaf? Then I understood. Listening to God's Word is not merely using our ears, but our hearts. I answered, "It would be tough, but I would."

The Lord then asked, "If you were mute, would you still praise My Name?"

How could I praise without a voice? Then it occurred to me: God wants us to sing from our very heart and soul. It never matters what we sound like. And praising God is not always with a song, but when we are persecuted, we give God praise with our words of thanks. So, I answered, "Though I could not physically sing, I would still praise Your Name."

And the Lord asked, "Do you really love Me?"

With courage and a strong conviction, I answered boldly, "Yes Lord! I love You because You are the one and true God!" I thought I had answered well.

But then God asked, "THEN WHY DO YOU SIN?"

I answered, "Because I am only human. I am not perfect."

"THEN WHY IN TIMES OF PEACE DO YOU STRAY THE FURTHEST? WHY ONLY IN TIMES OF TROUBLE DO YOU PRAY IN EARNEST?"

No answers. Only tears.

The Lord continued: "Why only sing at fellowships and retreats? Why seek Me only in times of worship? Why ask things so selfishly? Why ask things so unfaithfully?"

The tears continued to roll down my checks.

"Why are you ashamed of Me?"

"Why are you not spreading the Good News? Why in times of persecution, do you cry to others when I offer My shoulder to cry on? Why make excuses when I give you opportunities to serve in My Name?"

I tried to answer, but there was no answer to give.

"You are blessed with life. I did not make you to throw this gift away. I have blessed you with talents to serve Me, but you continue to turn away. I have revealed My word to you, but you do not gain in knowledge. I have spoken to you, but your ears were closed. I have shown My blessings to you, but your eyes were turned away. I have sent you servants, but you sat idly by as they were pushed away. I have heard your prayers and I have answered them all."

"DO YOU TRULY LOVE ME?"

I could not answer. How could I? I was embarrassed beyond belief. I had no excuse. What could I say to this? When my heart had cried out and the tears had flowed, I said, "Please forgive me Lord. I am unworthy to be Your child."

The Lord answered, "That is My grace, My child."

I asked, "Then why do you continue to forgive me? Why do You love me so?"

The Lord answered, "Because you are My creation. You are My child. I will never abandon you. When you cry, I will have compassion and cry with you. When you shout with joy, I will laugh with you. When you are down, I will encourage you. When you fall, I will raise you up. When you are tired, I will carry you."

"I will be with you till the end of days, and I will love you forever."

Never had I cried so hard before. How could I have been so cold? How could I have hurt God as I had done? I asked God, "How much do You love me?"

The Lord stretched out His arms, and I saw His nail-pierced hands. I bowed down at the feet of Christ, my Savior. And for the first time, I truly prayed.

Who's Your Daddy?

A number of years ago, a seminary professor was vacationing with his wife in Gatlinburg, Tennessee, where they were eating breakfast at a little restaurant, hoping to enjoy a quiet family meal. While they were waiting for their food, they noticed a distinguished looking, white-haired man moving from table to table visiting with the guests. The professor leaned over and whispered to his wife, "I hope he doesn't come over here."

But sure enough, the man did come over to their table. "Where are you folks from?" he asked in a friendly voice.

"Oklahoma," they answered.

"Great to have you here in Tennessee," the stranger said. "What do you do for a living?"

"I teach at a seminary," he replied.

"Oh, you teach preachers how to preach? Well, I've got a really great story for you." And with that, the gentleman pulled up a chair and sat down at the table with the couple.

"See that mountain over there?" (pointing out the restaurant window.) Not far from the base of that mountain, there was a boy born to an unwed mother. He had a hard time growing up, because every place he went, he was always asked the same question, 'Hey boy, who's your daddy?'

"Whether he was at school, in the grocery store or the drug store, people would ask the same question, 'Who's your daddy?' He would hide at recess and lunchtime from other students. He would avoid going in to stores because that question hurt him so bad.

"When he was about 12 years old, a new preacher came to his church. He would always go in late and slip out early to avoid people asking the question, 'Who's your daddy?' But one day, the new preacher said the benediction so fast he got caught and had to walk out with the crowd.

"Just about the time he got to the back door, the new preacher not knowing anything about him, put his hand on his shoulder and asked him, 'Son, who's your daddy?'

"The whole church got deathly quiet. He could feel every eye in the church looking at him. By now, everyone knew the answer to the question, 'Who's your daddy?'

"This new preacher, though, sensed the situation around him and using discernment that only the Holy Spirit could give, said the following to that scared little boy ...

"'Wait a minute!' he said, 'I know who you are. I see the family resemblance now. You are a child of God.'

"With that he patted the boy on his shoulder and said, 'Boy, you've got a great inheritance. Go and claim it.'

With that, the boy smiled for the first time in a long time and walked out the door a changed person. He was never the same again. Whenever anybody asked him, 'Who's your daddy?' he'd just tell them, 'I'm a child of God.'"

The distinguished gentleman got up from the table and said, "Isn't that a great story?"

The professor responded that it really was a great story!

As the man turned to leave, he said, "You know, if that new preacher hadn't told me that I was one of God's children, I probably never would have amounted to anything!" And he walked away.

The seminary professor and his wife were stunned. He called the waitress over and asked her, "Do you know who that man was who was sitting at our table and just left ?"

The waitress grinned and said, "Of course. Everybody here knows him. That's Ben Hooper. He's the former governor of Tennessee!"

"Let's Roll"
The Faith of Todd Beamer

"I don't think we're going to get out of this thing. I'm going to have to go out on faith."

It was the voice of Todd Beamer, the passenger ... and Wheaton College graduate ... who said, "Let's roll" as he led the charge against the terrorists who had hijacked United Flight 93—the one, you will remember, that crashed in the Pennsylvania countryside on September 11, 2001.

The whole world knows how brave Beamer and his fellow passengers were that day. We have now learned more fully what buttressed that bravery: Faith in Jesus Christ. Todd died as he lived: a faithful evangelical believer.

In an article titled "The Real Story of Flight 93," *Newsweek* reveals gripping new details from the actual transcripts of the now-recovered cockpit voice recorded. "Todd had been afraid," *Newsweek* relates. "More than once, he cried out for his Savior."

After passengers were herded to the back of the jet, Beamer called the GTE Customer Center in Oakbrook, Illinois. He told supervisor Lisa Jefferson about the hijacking. The passengers were planning to jump the terrorists, he said. And then he asked her to pray with him.

As *Newsweek* relates, "Beamer kept a Lord's Prayer bookmark in his Tom Clancy novel, but he didn't need any prompting. He began to recite the ancient litany, and Jefferson joined him: Our Father which art in heaven, hallowed be thy name."

As they finished, Beamer added, "Jesus, help me ..."

And then, Beamer and his fellow passengers prayed a prayer that has comforted millions down through the centuries. The prayer that David wrote in a time of great anguish: "The Lord is my shepherd, I shall now want ... yea, though I walk through the valley of the shadow of death, I will fear no evil."

And then the famous last words: "Are you guys ready? Let's roll."

We now know from the cockpit voice recorder, that Beamer and other passengers wrestled with the hijackers and forced the plane to crash into the ground, killing themselves, but foiling what was believed to have been the hijackers' plan to fly Flight 93 into the Capitol or the White House.

As Christians, we know that God can bring good out of evil. In Todd Beamer, the world witnessed a faith that held up in the extremity of fear—a faith that is even now comforting his widow and two young sons.

Lisa Beamer told NBC's *Dateline,* "You know, in the Lord's Prayer, it asks us to 'forgive our trespasses as we forgive those who trespass against us.' As Todd prayed this prayer in the last moments of his life, in a way," Lisa said, "he was forgiving those people for what they were doing, the most horrible thing you could ever do to someone."

It wasn't Todd Beamer's job to fight terrorists. He was just a passenger, who along with several others, did what he didn't have to do, but foiled a terrible evil that might have been done to his country.

As Flight 93 hurtled toward destruction, Todd Beamer could not have known that his quiet prayers would ultimately be heard by millions ... that the story of his last acts on earth would be a witness to the Lord he loved, serving as a lasting example of true heroism.

Church Chuckles

11

Just One More Laugh

Creative Creation
And That's Why …
In the Beginning

Theology 101
Adam and Eve's Marriage
The Bible in 50 Words
Noah and the Environmentalists

Who Is Jesus?
Three Proofs that Jesus Was …
Wanted: Jesus
Job Locator

The Gospel According to Kids
A Helping Hand from Above
I Am a Father
Out of the Mouths of Babes
Little Alex
Simple Wisdom

Church Life
You Might Be a Southern Baptist If ...
New Pastor's Visit
The Substitute Organist
Signs on Church Property
Church Ad Bloopers

The Pearly Gates
A Dead Engineer
Last Wish
God and Bill Gates

Church Humor
Freezing to Death
Light Bulbs
The Chauffeur
Nuts by the Fence

Just One More Laugh

The media pictures religious people as dour, fun-choking people who wag their fingers and act as moral police. They depict their lives as dull and dictated by a lot of silly rules.

But how wrong this stereotype is! God created humans with a sense of humor and an ability to laugh. These are precious gifts that we can enjoy over and over again. Without a doubt, Christians have more to laugh about than anyone else on earth. Our lives are full of joy and happiness.

Laughter is the best when we are laughing at ourselves. When we notice the little quirks and the odd incidents that fill our lives, we find ourselves chuckling, grinning, smiling, and belly-laughing.

Think back to a time when something you did made people laugh. Not the sneering, "I-see-that-you're stupid" kind of event, but one of those moments when you did something that just touched someone else's funny bone. Do you remember a time when you and a close friend heard a joke that made both of you bend over in laughter? Do you recall a moment when a child made a comment that made the whole room smile? Were any of these moments created in the midst of your church experience? Although we know when to be serious and strengthen our spiritual life, we also take time to laugh and enjoy the fellowship around the spiritual table.

This chapter has captured some of these moments. You can read them over and over again, chuckling anew each time you do. Then you can send a joke or two to your best cyberspace friends, enjoying the moment together in cybertime.

People complain that the Internet is choked with pornography and frustrating spam. We can change that in our corner of cyberspace. Fill your cyberwaves with fun and laughter. Bring a moment of joy to a friend who's slogging away at work, to a relative who's ill and can't get out, or to a parent who eagerly awaits a message from you. For just a moment, help them turn their attention to the spiritual side of life.

What are you waiting for? Don't keep the laughter to yourself! Share it with someone right now.

Creative Creation

And That's Why ...

Early on the fifth day of creation, God created the cow. He said to the cow, "Today I have created you! As a cow, you must go to the field and work all day long under the sun! I will give you a life span of 50 years."

The cow objected. "What? This kind of tough life you want me to live for 50 years? Let me have 20 years, and the 30 years I'll give back to you."

So God agreed.

On the same day, God created the dog. God said to the dog, "What you are supposed to do is to sit all day by the door of your house. Anything that comes in, you will have to bark at it! I'll give you a life span of 20 years."

The dog objected. "What? All day long to sit by the door? No way! I'll give you back my other 10 years of life!"

So God agreed.

By that evening, God created the monkey. He said to the monkey, "Monkeys have to be entertainers. You've got to make the man I create laugh by doing monkey tricks. I'll give you a 20-year life span."

The monkey objected. "What? Make man laugh? Do monkey faces and tricks? Ten years will do, and the other ten years I'll give you back."

So God agreed.

On the sixth day, God created man and said to him, "Your job is to sleep, eat, and play. You will enjoy things very much in your life. All you need to do is just enjoy and do nothing. For this kind of life, I'll give you a 20-year life span."

The man objected. "What? Such a good life! Eat, play, sleep, do nothing? Enjoy the best and you expect me to live for only 20 years? No way, man! Why don't we make a deal? Since the cow gave you back 30 years, and the dog gave you back 10 years and the monkey gave you back 10 years, I will take them from you! That makes my life span 70 years, right?"

So God agreed.

And that's why ...

In our first 20 years, we eat, sleep, play, enjoy the best and do nothing much. For the next 30 years, we work all day long, suffer, and get to support the family. For the next ten years, we entertain our grandchildren by making monkey faces and doing monkey tricks. And for the last ten years, we stay at home, sit by the front door, and bark at people!

In the Beginning

In the beginning, God created the heavens and the earth. And the earth was without form, and void, and darkness was upon the face of the deep.

And Satan said, "It doesn't get any better than this."

And God said, "Let there be light," and there was light. And God said, "Let the earth bring forth grass, the herb yielding seed, and the fruit tree yielding fruit," and God saw that it was good.

And Satan said, "There goes the neighborhood."

And God said, "Let us make Man in our image, after our likeness, and let them have dominion over the fish of the sea, and over the fowl of the air and over the cattle, and over all the Earth, and over every creeping thing that creepth upon the Earth." And so God created Man in His own image; male and female created He them. And God looked upon Man and Woman and saw that they were lean and fit.

And Satan said, "I know how I can get back in this game."

And God populated the earth with broccoli and cauliflower and spinach, green and yellow vegetables of all kinds, so Man and Woman would live long and healthy lives.

And Satan created McDonald's. And McDonalds brought forth the 99-cent double cheeseburger. And Satan said to Man, "You want fries with that?"

And Man said, "Supersize them." And Man gained five pounds.

And God created the healthful yogurt so that Woman might keep her figure that Man found so fair.

And Satan brought forth chocolate. And Woman gained five pounds.

And God said, "Try my crispy fresh salad."

And Satan brought forth Ben and Jerry's. And Woman gained ten pounds.

And God said, "I have sent thee heart-healthy vegetables and olive oil with which to cook them."

And Satan brought forth chicken-fried steak so big that it needed its own platter. And Man gained 10 pounds and his bad cholesterol went through the roof.

And God brought forth running shoes, and Man resolved to lose those extra pounds.

And Satan brought forth cable TV with remote control, so that Man would not have to toil to change channels between ESPN and ESPN2. And Man gained another 20 pounds.

And God said, "You're running up the score, Devil." And God brought forth the potato, a vegetable naturally low in fat and brimming with nutrition.

And Satan peeled off the healthy skin and sliced the starchy center into chips and deep-fat fried them. And he created sour cream dip, also. And Man clutched his remote control and ate the potato chips swaddled in cholesterol. And Satan saw and said, "It is good." And Man went into cardiac arrest. And God sighed and created quadruple bypass surgery. And Satan created HMOs.

Theology 101

Adam and Eve's Marriage

Adam and Eve had an ideal marriage. He didn't have to hear about all the men she could have married, and she didn't have to hear about the way his mother cooked.

The Bible in 50 Words

God made.
Adam bit.
Noah arked.
Abraham split.
Joseph ruled.
Jacob fooled.
Bush talked.
Moses balked.
Pharaoh plagued.
People walked.
Sea divided.
Tablets guided.
Promise landed.
Saul freaked.
David peeked.
Prophets warned.

Jesus born.
God walked.
Love talked.
Anger crucified.
Hope died.
Love rose.
Spirit flamed.
Word spread.
God remained.

God Bless You!

Noah and the Environmentalists

If Noah had lived in the United States in the year 2006, the story may have gone something like this:

And the Lord spoke to Noah and said, "In one year, I am going to make it rain and cover the whole earth with water until all flesh is destroyed. But I want you to save the righteous people and two of every kind of living thing on earth. Therefore, I am commanding you to build an Ark."

In a flash of lightning, God delivered the specifications for an Ark. In fear and trembling, Noah took the plans and agreed to build the Ark. "Remember," said the Lord, "you must complete the Ark and bring everything aboard in one year."

Exactly one year later, fierce storm clouds covered the earth and all the seas went into a turmoil. The Lord saw that Noah was sitting in his front yard weeping.

"Noah!" He shouted. "Where is the Ark?"

"Lord, please forgive me," cried Noah. "I did my best, but there were big problems. First, I had to get a permit for construction, and Your plans did not meet the building codes. I had to hire an engineering firm and redraw the plans. Then I got into a fight with OSHA over whether or not the Ark needed a sprinkler system and approved floatation devices.

"Then, my neighbor objected, claiming I was violating zoning ordinances by building the Ark in my front yard, so I had to get a variance from the city planning commission.

"I had problems getting enough wood for the Ark because there was a ban on cutting trees to protect the spotted owl. I finally convinced the US Forest Service that I really needed the wood to save the owls. However, the Fish and Wildlife Service won't let me take the two owls.

"The carpenters formed a union and went on strike. I had to negotiate a settlement with the National Labor Relations Board before anyone would pick up a saw or hammer. Now, I have 16 carpenters on the Ark, but still no owls. When I started rounding up the other animals, an animal rights group sued me. They objected to me taking only two of each kind aboard. This suit is pending.

"Meanwhile, the EPA notified me that I could not complete the Ark without filing an environmental impact statement on Your proposed flood. They didn't take very kindly to the idea that they had no jurisdiction over the conduct of the Creator of the universe. Then, the Army Corps of Engineers demanded a map of the proposed flood plain. I sent them a globe.

"Right now, I am trying to resolve a complaint filed with the Equal Employment Opportunity Commission that I am practicing discrimination by not taking atheists aboard. The IRS has seized my assets, claiming that I'm building the Ark in preparation to flee the country to avoid paying taxes. I just got a notice from the state that I owe them some kind of user tax and failed to register the Ark as a 'recreational water craft.'

"And finally, the ACLU got the courts to issue an injunction against further construction of the Ark, saying that since God is flooding the earth, it's a religious event, and, therefore unconstitutional. I really don't think I can finish the Ark for another five or six years."

Noah waited. The sky began to clear, the sun began to shine, and the seas began to calm. A rainbow arced across the sky. Noah looked up hopefully. "You mean you're not going to destroy the earth, Lord?"

"No," He said sadly. "I don't have to. The government already has."

Who Is Jesus?

Three Proofs that Jesus Was ...

Someone said there were three proofs that Jesus was ... Mexican.
1. His first name was Jesus.
2. He was bilingual.
3. He was always being harassed by the authorities.

But then there were equally good arguments that Jesus was ... black.
1. He went into His Father's business.
2. He lived at home until He was 30.
3. He was sure His Mother was a virgin, and His mother was sure He was God.

But then there were equally good arguments that Jesus was ... Italian.
1. He talked with His hands.
2. He had wine with every meal.
3. He used olive oil.

But then there were equally good arguments that Jesus was …
a Californian.

1. He never cut his hair.
2. He walked around barefoot.
3. He started a new religion.

But then there were equally good arguments that Jesus was …
Irish.

1. He never got married.
2. He was always telling stories.
3. He loved green pastures.

But perhaps the most compelling evidence …
Three proofs that Jesus was … a woman.

1. He had to feed a crowd at a moment's notice when there was
no food.

2. He kept trying to get the message across to a bunch of men
who JUST DIDN'T GET IT.

3. Even when He was dead, He had to get up because there
was more work for Him to do.

Wanted: Jesus

If Jesus did His same ministry on earth over again today, He
would be wanted by …

… the **ATF** for turning water into wine without a license,

… the **EPA** for killing fig trees,

… the **AMA** for practicing medicine without a license,

… the **County Coroner** for asking people to open graves and
for raising the dead,

… the **Health Department** for feeding 5,000 people in the
wilderness,

… the **NEA** for teaching without a certificate,

... **OSHA** for walking on water without a life-jacket and for flying without an airplane,

... the **SPCA** for driving hogs into the sea,

... the **National Board of Psychiatry** for giving advice on how to live a guilt-free life,

... **NOW** for not choosing a woman apostle,

... the **Abortion Rights League** for saying that if a person harms children, it is better that he had never been born,

... the **Inter-Faith Movement** for condemning all other religions,

... and though He is a carpenter, by the **Zoning Department** for building mansions without a permit.

Job Locator

To: Jesus, Son of Joseph. Woodcrafters shop. Nazareth
From: Jordan Management Consultants. Jerusalem.
Subject: Staff Aptitude Test.
Date: May 2, 30 AD

Thank you for submitting the resumes of the 12 men you picked for management positions in your new organization. All of them have now taken our battery of tests, and we have not only run the results through our computer, but also have arranged personal interviews for each of them with our psychologist and vocational consultant.

It is the staff opinion that most of your nominees are lacking in background, education, and vocational aptitude for the type of enterprise you are undertaking. They do not have the team concept. We would recommend that you continue your search for persons of expertise in managerial ability and proven capability.

Simon Peter is emotionally unstable and given to fits of temper. Andrew has absolutely no qualities of leadership. The two brothers,

James and John, the sons of Zebedee, place personal interest above company loyalty. Thomas demonstrates a questioning attitude that would tend to undermine morale.

We feel that it is our duty to tell you that Matthew has been blacklisted by the Greater Jerusalem Better Business Bureau. James, the son of Alphaeus, and Thaddeus definitely have radical leanings, and they both registered a high score on the manic-depressive scale.

One of the candidates, however, shows great potential. He is a man of ability and resourcefulness, meets people well, has a keen business mind, and has contacts in high places. He is highly motivated, ambitious, and innovative. We recommend Judas Iscariot as your controller and right-hand man. All other profiles are self-explanatory.

We wish you every success in your new venture.

The Gospel According to Kids

A Helping Hand from Above

A priest is walking down the street one day when he notices a very small boy trying to press a doorbell on a house across the street. However, the boy is very small and the doorbell is too high for him to reach.

After watching the boy's efforts for some time, the priest moves closer to the boy's position. He steps smartly across the street, walks up behind the little fellow and, placing his hand kindly on the child's shoulder, leans over and gives the doorbell a solid ring.

Crouching down to the child's level, the priest smiles benevolently and asks, "And now what, my little man?"

To which the boy replies, "Now we run like hell!"

I Am a Father

A little boy got on the bus, sat next to a man reading a book, and noticed he had his collar on backwards. The little boy asked why he wore his collar that way.

The man, who was a priest, said, "I am a Father."

The little boy replied, "My Daddy doesn't wear his collar like that."

The priest looked up from his book and answered, "I am the Father of many."

The boy said, "My Dad has four boys, four girls and two grandchildren, and he doesn't wear his collar that way."

The priest, getting impatient, said, "I am the Father of hundreds," and went back to reading his book.

The little boy sat quietly, but on leaving the bus he leaned over and said, "Well, maybe you should wear your pants backwards instead of your collar."

Out of the Mouths of Babes

A Sunday school teacher was teaching her class about the difference between right and wrong. "All right, children, let's take another example," she said. "If I were to get into a man's pocket and take his billfold with all his money, what would I be?"

Little Johnny raises his hand, and with a confident smile, he blurts out, "You'd be his wife!"

* * *

A Sunday school teacher asked the children just before she dismissed them to go to church, "And why is it necessary to be quiet in church?"

Annie replied, "Because people are sleeping."

* * *

A Sunday school teacher asked her class why Joseph and Mary took Jesus with them to Jerusalem.

A small child replied, "They couldn't get a baby-sitter."

* * *

A Sunday school teacher was discussing the Ten Commandments with her five- and six-year olds. After explaining the commandment to "honor thy father and thy mother," she asked, "Is there a commandment that teaches us how to treat our brothers and sisters?"

Without missing a beat, one little boy answered, "Thou shall not kill."

* * *

At Sunday school, the teacher was teaching how God created everything, including human beings. Little Johnny seemed especially intent when she told him how Eve was created out of one of Adam's ribs.

Later in the week, his mother noticed him lying down as though he were ill and said, "Johnny what is the matter?"

Little Johnny responded, "I have a pain in my side. I think I'm going to have a wife."

Little Alex

One Sunday morning, the pastor noticed that little Alex was staring up at the large plaque that hung in the foyer of the church. The plaque was covered with names, and small American flags were mounted on either side of it. The little seven-year-old had been staring at the plaque for some time, so the pastor walked up, stood beside the boy, and said quietly, "Good morning, Alex."

"Good morning, pastor," replied the young man, still focused on the plaque.

"Pastor Jamison, what is this?" Alex asked.

"Well, son, it's a memorial to all the young men and women who died in the service."

Soberly, they stood together, staring at the large plaque. Little Alex's voice was barely audible when he asked, "Which service, the 9:00 or the 11:00?"

Simple Wisdom

A young liberal teacher proudly explained to her class of small children that she was an atheist. She asked if they were atheists too. Not knowing what atheism is, most of the kids raised their hands.

Little Lucy, however, did not go along with the crowd. The teacher asked her why she didn't raise her hand.

"Because I'm not an atheist. I'm a Christian!" said Lucy.

"Why are you a Christian?" asked the red-faced teacher.

"Well," said Lucy, "I was brought up knowing and loving Jesus. My Mom is a Christian, and my Dad is a Christian, so I am a Christian."

The teacher said angrily, "That's no reason. What if your parents were idiots. What would you be then?"

"An atheist," said Lucy.

Church Life

You Might Be a Southern Baptist If ...

1. You believe you are supposed to take a covered dish to Heaven.

2. You have never sung the third verse of any hymn.

3. You have ever put an IOU in the collection plate.

4. You think that someone who says "amen" while the pastor is preaching is charismatic.

5. You complain because your pastor only works one day a week, and then he works too long.

6. You clapped in church last Sunday and felt guilty all week.

7. You woke up craving fried chicken one morning and interpreted it as a call to preach.

8. You are old enough to get Senior Citizen's discounts at the pharmacy, but not old enough to be promoted into the Senior Adult Department.

9. You think the epistles are probably the apostle's wives.

10. You think the Holy Land is Nashville.

11. You think God's presence is always strongest in the back three pews.

12. You think John the Baptist founded the Southern Baptist Convention.

13. You think *Victory in Jesus* is the national anthem.

14. The first complete sentence you uttered was "We've never done it this way before."

15. You judge the quality of the sermon by the amount of sweat worked up by the preacher.

16. Your definition of fellowship has something to do with food.

17. You honestly believe the apostle Paul spoke King James English.

18. You think worship service music has to be loud.

19. You think Jesus actually used Welch's grape juice and unsalted crackers.

20. You think preachers who wear robes are in cahoots with the Catholics.

(Greg Hartman, Christian Humor Guide, www.christianhumor.about.com)

New Pastor's Visit

A new pastor who moved into town went out one Saturday to visit his parishioners. All went well until he came to one house. It was obvious that someone was home, but no one came to the door even after he had knocked several times. Finally, he took out his card, wrote on the back "Revelation 3:20" and stuck it in the door.

The next day, as he was counting the offering, he found his card in the collection plate. Below his message was the notation "Genesis 3:10."

Now Revelation 3:20 reads: "Behold, I stand at the door and knock. If any man hear my voice, and opens the door, I will come in to him, and will dine with him, and he with me." And Genesis 3:10 reads: "And he said, I heard thy voice in the garden, and I was afraid, because I was naked."

The Substitute Organist

The minister was preoccupied with thoughts of how he was going to ask the congregation to come up with more money than they were expecting for repairs to the church building. Therefore, he was annoyed to find that the regular organist was sick and a substitute had been brought in at the last minute. The substitute wanted to know what to play.

"Here's a copy of the service," he said impatiently. "But you'll have to think of something to play after I make the announcement about the finances."

During the service, the minister paused and said, "Brothers and Sisters, we are in great difficulty; the roof repairs cost twice as much as we expected, and we need $4,000 more. Any of you who can pledge $100 or more, please stand up."

At the moment, the substitute organist played *The Star Spangled Banner*.

And that is how the substitute became the regular organist!

Signs on Church Property

- "No God—No Peace. Know God—Know Peace"
- "Free Trip to Heaven. Details Inside!"
- "Try Our Sundays. They Are Better Than Baskin-Robbins."
- "Searching for a New Look? Have Your Faith Lifted Here!"
- "People Are Like Tea Bags. You Have to Put Them in Hot Water Before You Know How Strong They Are."
- "When Down in the Mouth, Remember Jonah. He Came Out All Right."
- "Fight Truth Decay. Study the Bible Daily."
- "How Will You Spend Eternity? Smoking or Nonsmoking?"
- "Dusty Bibles Lead to Dirty Lives."
- "Come Work for the Lord. The Work is Hard, the Hours are Long and the Pay is Low. But the Retirement Benefits are Out of This World."
- "It Is Unlikely There'll Be a Reduction in the Wages of Sin."
- "Do Not Wait for the Hearse to Bring You to Church."
- "If You Are Headed in the Wrong Direction, God Allows U-turns."
- "If You Don't Like the Way You Were Born, Try Being Born Again."
- "Looking at the Way Some People Live, They Ought to Obtain Eternal Fire Insurance."
- "This is a Ch__ch. What Is Missing?" (U R)
- "Forbidden Fruit Creates Many Jams."
- "In the Dark? Follow the Son."
- "Running Low on Faith? Stop In for a Fill-up."
- "If You Can't Sleep, Don't Count Sheep. Talk to the Shepherd."

"A merry heart doeth good like a medicine" (Proverbs 17:22).

Church Ad Bloopers

These are actual clippings from church newspapers. It's amazing what a little proofreading could've prevented.

Bertha Belch, a missionary from Africa, will be speaking tonight at The Calvary Memorial Church in Racine. Come tonight and hear Bertha Belch all the way from Africa.

* * *

Don't forget the National Prayer and Fasting Conference. "The cost for attending the Fasting and Prayer conference includes meals."

* * *

Our youth basketball team is back in action Wednesday at 8 PM in the school recreation hall. Come out and watch us kill Christ the King.

* * *

Miss Charlene Mason sang, "I Will Not Pass This Way Again," giving obvious pleasure to the congregation.

* * *

Ladies, don't forget the rummage sale. It's a chance to get rid of those things not worth keeping around the house. Don't forget your husbands.

* * *

Next Sunday is the family hayride and bonfire at the Fowlers'. Bring your own hot dogs and guns. Friends are welcome! Everyone come for a fun time.

* * *

The peacemaking meeting scheduled for today has been canceled due to a conflict.

* * *

The sermon this morning: "Jesus Walks on the Water." The sermon tonight will be: "Searching for Jesus."

* * *

Barbara Jones remains in the hospital and needs blood donors for more transfusions. She is also having trouble sleeping and requests tapes of Pastor Jack's sermons.

* * *

The Rector will preach his farewell message after which the choir will sing "Break Forth into Joy."

* * *

Remember in prayer the many who are sick of our community. Smile at someone who is hard to love. Say "hell" to someone who doesn't care much about you, and hopefully they will respond.

* * *

Don't let worry kill you. Let the Church help.

* * *

Irving Benson and Jessica Carter were married on October 24 in the church. So ends a friendship that began in their school days.

* * *

At the evening service tonight, the sermon will be "What is Hell?" Come early and listen to our choir practice.

* * *

Eight new choir robes are currently needed due to the addition of several new members and to the deterioration of some older ones.

* * *

The senior choir invites any member of the congregation who enjoys sinning to join the choir.

* * *

Scouts are saving aluminum cans, bottles, and other items to be recycled. Proceeds will be used to cripple children.

* * *

The Lutheran men's group will meet at 6 PM. Steak, mashed potatoes, green beans, bread, and dessert will be served for a nominal feel.

* * *

For those of you who have children and don't know it, we have a nursery downstairs.

* * *

The church will host an evening of fine dining, superb entertainment, and gracious hostility.

* * *

Potluck supper Sunday at 5:00 P.M. Prayer and medication to follow.

* * *

The ladies of the Church have cast off clothing of every kind. They may be seen in the basement on Friday afternoon.

* * *

This evening at 7 P.M. there will be a hymn sing in the park across from the Church. Bring a blanket and come prepared to sin.

* * *

The pastor would appreciate it if the ladies of the congregation would lend him their electric girdles for the pancake breakfast next Sunday morning.

* * *

Low Self Esteem Support Group will meet Thursday at 8 P.M. Please use the back door.

* * *

The eighth-graders will be presenting Shakespeare's "Hamlet" in the Church basement on Friday at 7 P.M. The Congregation is invited to attend this tragedy.

* * *

Weight Watches will meet at 7 P.M. at the First Presbyterian Church. Please use the large double door at the side entrance.

The Pearly Gates

A Dead Engineer

An engineer dies and reports to the pearly gates. St. Peter checks his dossier and says, "Ah, you're an engineer. You're in the wrong place."

So, the engineer reports to the gates of hell and is let in.

Pretty soon, the engineer gets dissatisfied with the level of comfort in hell and starts designing and building improvements.

After a while, they've got air conditioning, flush toilets and escalators, and the engineer is a pretty popular guy.

One day God calls Satan up on the telephone and says with a sneer, "So, how's it going down there in hell?"

Satan replied, "Hey, things are going great. We've got air conditioning, flush toilets and escalators, and there's no telling what this engineer is going to come up with next."

God replies, "What??? You've got an engineer? That's a mistake! He should never have gotten down there; send him up here."

Satan says, "No way. I like having an engineer on the staff, and I'm keeping him."

God says, "Send him back up here or I'll sue."

Satan laughs uproariously and answers, "Yeah, right. And just where are YOU going to get a lawyer?"

Last Wish

Two priests died at the same time and met Saint Peter at the Pearly Gates. Saint Peter said, "I'd like to let you guys in now, but our computer is down. You'll have to go back to Earth for about a week, but you can't go back as priests. So what else would you like to be?"

The first priest says, "I've always wanted to be an eagle, soaring above the Rocky Mountains."

"So be it," says Saint Peter, and off flies the first priest.

The second priest mulls this over for a moment and asks, "Will any of this week 'count,' Saint Peter?"

"No, I told you the computer's down. There's no way we can keep track of what you're doing."

"In that case," says the second priest, "I've always wanted to be a stud."

"So be it," says Saint Peter, and the second priest disappears.

A week goes by, the computer is fixed, and the Lord tells Saint Peter to recall the two priests. "Will you have any trouble locating them?" he asks.

"The first one should be easy," says Saint Peter. "He's somewhere over the Rockies, flying with the eagles. But the second one could prove to be more difficult."

"Why?" asks the Lord.

"He's on a snow tire, somewhere in North Dakota."

God and Bill Gates

Bill Gates died in a car accident. He found himself in Purgatory being sized up by God. "Well, Bill, I'm really confused on this call. I'm not sure whether to send you to heaven or hell. After all, you enormously helped society by putting a computer in almost every home in the world, and yet you created that ghastly Windows 2000. I'm going to do something I've never done before. In your case, I'm going to let you decide where you want to go!"

Bill replied, "Well, thanks, God. What's the difference between the two?"

God said, "I'm willing to let you visit both places briefly if it will help you make the decision."

"Fine, but where should I go first?"

God said, "I'm going to leave that up to you."

Bill said, "OK, then, let's try hell first." So Bill went to hell. It was a beautiful, clean, sandy beach with clear waters. There were thousands of beautiful women running around, playing in the water, laughing and frolicking about. The sun was shining, the temperature was perfect. Bill was very pleased. "This is great!" he told God. "If this is hell, I REALLY want to see heaven!"

"Fine," said God and off they went. Heaven was a high place in clouds with angels drifting about playing harps and singing. It was nice but not as enticing as hell.

Bill thought for a quick minute and rendered his decision. "Hmm, I think I prefer hell," he told God.

"Fine," retorted God, "as you desire." So Bill Gates went to hell.

Two weeks later, God decided to check up on the late billionaire to see how he was doing in hell. When God arrived in hell, he found Bill shackled to a wall, screaming amongst the hot flames in a dark cave. He was being burned and tortured by demons.

"How's everything going, Bill?" God asked.

Bill responded, his voice full of anguish and disappointment, "This is awful. This is not what I expected. I can't believe this happened. What happened to that other place with the beaches and the beautiful women playing in the water?"

God says, "That was just the screen saver."

Church Humor

Freezing to Death

Two men waiting at the Pearly Gates strike up a conversation.
"How'd you die?" the first man asks the second.
"I froze to death," says the second.
"That's awful," says the first man.
"How does it feel to freeze to death?"
"It's very uncomfortable at first," says the second man. "You get the shakes, and you get pains in all your fingers and toes. But eventually, it's a very calm way to go. You get numb and you kind of drift off, as if you're sleeping. How about you, how did you die?"
"I had a heart attack," says the first man.
"You see, I knew my wife was cheating on me, so one day I showed up at home unexpectedly. I ran up to the bedroom and found her alone, knitting. I ran down to the basement, but no one was hiding there. I ran up to the second floor, but no one was hiding there either. I ran as fast as I could to the attic, and just as I got there, I had a massive heart attack and died."
The second man shakes his head. "That's so ironic," he says.
"What do you mean?" asks the first man.
"If you had only stopped to look in the freezer, we'd both still be alive."

Light Bulbs

How many Christians does it take to change a light bulb?

Charismatics: Only one. Hands are already in the air.
Pentecostals: Ten. One to change the bulb, and nine to pray against the spirit of darkness.

Presbyterians: None. Lights will go on and off at predestined times.

Roman Catholic: None. Candles only.

Baptists: At least 15. One to change the light bulb, and three committees to approve the change and decide who brings the potato salad.

Episcopalians: Eight. One to call the electrician, and seven to say how much they liked the old one better.

Mormons: Five. One man to change the bulb, and four wives to tell him how to do it.

Unitarians: We choose not to make a statement either in favor of or against the need for a light bulb. However, if in your own journey you have found that light bulbs work for you, that is fine. You are invited to write a poem or compose a modern dance about your personal relationship with your light bulb, and present it next month at our annual light bulb Sunday service, in which we will explore a number of light bulb traditions, including incandescent, fluorescent, three-way, long-life and tinted, all of which are equally valid paths to luminescence.

Methodists: Undetermined. Whether your light is bright, dull, or completely out, you are loved, you can be a light bulb, turnip bulb, or tulip bulb. Church-wide lighting service is planned for Sunday, August 19. Bring bulb of your choice and a covered dish.

Nazarene: Six. One woman to replace the bulb while five men review church lighting policy.

Amish: What's a light bulb?

The Chauffeur

The Billy Graham crusade had just finished a tour of the Florida East Coast and was taking a limousine to the airport. Having never driven a limo, Billy Graham asked the chauffeur if he could drive for a while. Well, the chauffeur didn't have much of a choice, so he got in the back of the limo and Billy took the wheel.

Billy Graham turned onto I-95 and accelerated to about 90 MPH. WHAM! The blue lights of the State Highway Patrol flashed in his rearview mirror. He pulled over and a trooper came to his window.

When the trooper saw who it was, he said, "Just a moment, please, I need to call in."

The trooper radioed in and asked for the chief. He said, "I have a REALLY important person pulled over and I need to know what to do."

The chief replied, "Who is it, not Ted Kennedy again?"

The trooper said, "No, even more important."

"It isn't Governor Jeb Bush, is it?" asked the chief.

"No, even more important," replied the trooper.

"It isn't President George Bush, is it?"

"No," replied the trooper, "even more important."

"Well, WHO in the WORLD is it?" screamed the chief.

The trooper responded, "I don't know for sure, but I think it might be Jesus because his chauffeur is Billy Graham!"

Nuts by the Fence

On the outskirts of a small town, there was a big, old pecan tree just inside the cemetery fence. One day, two boys filled up a bucketful of nuts and sat down by the tree, out of sight, and began dividing them.

"One for you, one for me. One for you, one for me," said one boy.

Several dropped and rolled down toward the fence. Another boy came riding along the road on his bicycle. As he passed, he thought he heard voices from inside the cemetery. He slowed down to investigate. Sure enough, he heard, "One for you, one for me. One for you, one for me." He just knew what it was.

"Oh my," he shuddered, "it's Satan and the Lord dividing the souls at the cemetery." He jumped back on his bike and rode off.

Just around the bend, he met an old man with a cane, hobbling along. "Come here quick," said the boy. "You won't believe what I heard! Satan and the Lord are down at the cemetery dividing up the souls."

The man said, "Beat it, kid, can't you see it's hard for me to walk?" When the boy insisted though, the man hobbled to the cemetery. Standing by the fence they heard, "One for you, one for me … "

The old man whispered, "Boy, you've been telling the truth. Let's see if we can see the Lord himself." Shaking with fear, they peered through the fence, yet were still unable to see anything. The old man and the boy gripped the wrought iron bars of the fence tighter and tighter as they tried to get a glimpse of the Lord.

At last, they heard, "One for you, one for me." And one last, "One for you, one for me. That's all. Now let's go get those nuts by the fence, and we'll be done."

… They say the old man made it back to town a full five minutes ahead of the boy on the bike!

About the Authors

David W. Balsiger is the author of 39 literary works including 23 nonfiction books. Some of his better known books include *In Search of Noah's Ark* (Sunn), *The Lincoln Conspiracy* (New American Library), *The Incredible Power of Prayer* (Tyndale, 1998), *Ancient Secrets of the Bible* (Dell, 1994), *The Incredible Discovery of Noah's Ark* (Dell, 1995), *Face in the Mirror* (Bridge-Logos, 1993), and *The Evidence for Heaven* (Bridge-Logos, 2005). Three of his previous books were million-copy bestsellers including *The Lincoln Conspiracy, In Search of Noah's Ark*, and *The Satan Seller.* He is listed in 19 achievement directories including eight of the prestigious Marquis library directories. Mr. Balsiger is also the recipient of an honorary doctoral degree from Lincoln Memorial University (Harrogate, Tennessee) for the research contained in his book, *The Lincoln Conspiracy,* a 1977 book that was on the *New York Times* Best Sellers List for 22 weeks.

Christine C. Strong is a naturopathic physician who practices medical aesthetic procedures in Flagstaff, Arizona. She is an aspiring writer who is also coauthoring with David Balsiger a new book entitled *The Longevity Diet: How to Live to 100.* She is a member of the Arizona Naturopathic Medical Association.